4/25/16

D0780131

WITHDRAWN

MODERN PATHFINDERS:
Creating Better Research Guides

by
Jason Puckett

Association of College and Research Libraries
A division of the American Library Association
Chicago, Illinois 2015

The paper used in this publication meets the minimum requirements of American National Standard for Information Sciences–Permanence of Paper for Printed Library Materials, ANSI Z39.48-1992. ∞

Names: Puckett, Jason, 1969- author.
Title: Modern pathfinders : creating better research guides / by Jason Puckett.
Description: Chicago : Association of College and Research Libraries, a division of the American Library Association, 2015.
Identifiers: LCCN 2015037946| ISBN 9780838988176 (pbk.) | ISBN 9780838988183 (pdf) | ISBN 9780838988190 (epub) | ISBN 9780838988206 (kindle)
Subjects: LCSH: Electronic reference services (Libraries) | Research--Methodology--Web-based instruction. | Library orientation--Web-based instruction. | Web-based instruction--Design. | Web-based instruction--Evaluation. | Library Web sites--Design. | Libraries--Special collections--Electronic information resources. | School librarian participation in curriculum planning. | Academic libraries--Relations with faculty and curriculum.
Classification: LCC Z711.45 P83 2015 | DDC 001.4/202854678--dc23 LC record available at http://lccn.loc.gov/2015037946

Printed in the United States of America.

19 18 17 16 15 5 4 3 2 1

Table of Contents

Acknowledgments

No book is written in isolation, and I certainly wouldn't have been able to get this one done on my own.

First and last, thank you to my editor Kathryn Deiss. She's not only extraordinarily smart and competent, she's been patient and generous beyond measure when I've stumbled while writing this book. Kathryn, you are the best editor in libraryland.

Rachel Borchardt and Sarah Steiner are not only two of the best instruction librarians I know, but are my go-to manuscript readers. They both spotted angles I missed, helped me untangle tortured paragraphs, and called me out when I tried to get lazy and gloss over sections that needed more work. Not to mention giving me a verbal kick whenever I thought I'd never finish. Thank you both.

I'm indebted to Aaron Dobbs for agreeing to write the foreword and for his comments on this work. He's co-editor of the LITA Guide *Using Lib-Guides to Enhance Library Services*, which was invaluable to me for ideas and inspiration and should really be on your bookshelf next to this one. I'm looking forward to the next volume in the series.

As always, this book is for Anne, for mom and dad, and for Valerie and Ip.

Foreword

WHAT DO LIBRARIES DO? Broadly, libraries collect, evaluate, organize, and recommend information and information sources. The format of libraries' attempts to make finding stuff easier has adapted to the technologies available; pathfinders have morphed to include annotated lists, bibliographies, and online research guides. Research guides have the potential to improve the research experience of today's users (whether they are first-year students, experienced upperclass- or graduate students, budding researchers, faculty looking for effective routes to include information literacy in their course assignments, or John Q. Public) as they work their way through the library research process. Research is not an easy process, especially when looking for exhaustive, authoritative sources. Well-designed, cohesive research guides can improve the research experience by providing effective direction toward relevant resources and away, or around, less appropriate tools.

Modern Pathfinders: Creating better research guides provides a wide array of ideas worth thinking about, including recommendations for accommodating learning styles, incorporating solid user experience techniques, and making design and content decisions with a focus on learning theory. Jason covers theoretical underpinnings of design, use, and usability of research guides and goes beyond practical, applied suggestions for any one particular platform with effective and easy-to-incorporate suggestions for implementation.

There have been numerous article-length publications talking about pathfinders and a few book-length publications addressing specific platforms for creation and maintenance of research guides, each interesting within its specific focus area. This book-length treatment of pathfinders, writ large, is excellent for both the newer research guide designer and the old hand who has done web pages for years. The coherent fusion of instruction theory, learning styles, and user experience, in the first half of the book, integrates theory with practical application and provides a framework for improving existing or implementing research guides in libraries.

The topics covered in the latter half of this book, design, assessment, and administration, are only rarely covered together. If you, or perhaps a recalcitrant colleague, wonder about the usefulness of online pathfinders, reading these latter chapters and intentionally implementing even just one of the provided suggestions relevant to your situation or project should offer an effective path to follow for building a more effective user experience. Intentionally developing success metrics at the beginning of the project and building in measures to assess the effectiveness of your guides will provide supporting data and will also allow for focus on underperforming assets.

I've been following Jason's ideas on library instruction and libraryland in general for over a decade and highly recommend pretty much everything he's said in this arena. He's been a prolific presenter on library instruction, bibliographic citation management, and library technology. He writes fun, funny, and spot-on things online, he's co-hosted his own podcast—*Adventures in Library Instruction*, keynoted internationally, and presented in LYRASIS & ACRL webcasts. In writing *Modern Pathfinders: Creating better research guides*, Jason brings together and provides practical guidance for blending instructional theory, user experience, learning styles, and web design in one readable source. Leaning on ideas from this book, I will be re-evaluating my research guides with an eye toward improving their usefulness and usability. I hope you find useful ideas in Jason's writing, as I did, and I wish all of us well in our continuing quests to improve the research experience for our users.

—Aaron W. Dobbs
Scholarly Communication & Electronic Resources Librarian
Shippensburg University of Pennsylvania

Co-editor: *Using LibGuides to Enhance Online Library Services* (2011) *Integrating LibGuides in Library Websites* (2016), & *Innovative LibGuides Applications: Real World Examples* (2016); Editor: *The Library Assessment Cookbook* (2016)

Introduction

LIBRARIANS HAVE BEEN USING research guides in one form or another for a long time, as printed handouts that could be shared with classes or at the reference desk. Many, perhaps most, libraries have by now transitioned from using paper-based research guides to providing this kind of information via specialized webpages.

What's different about creating guides on the Web? Web-based research guides

- don't just provide information: they can serve as active research tools, with links, search boxes, and other interactive elements;
- are infinitely discoverable (even by users who aren't aware that the library provides them) via web searches;
- are available any time of the day, when your library is closed, to researchers from inside and outside your constituency, who never set foot in the library or speak to a reference librarian;
- can be updated easily as users' needs change, as assessment reveals potential improvements, and as research tools change;
- contain content that can be shared and reused among guide authors and repurposed by other libraries;
- can be created collaboratively by multiple librarians and even faculty members;
- can include multimedia elements like audio and video and self-updating elements like RSS feeds; and
- benefit from a working knowledge of how to write well for the web (studies show that we read web content differently from print content).

About This Book

This book is primarily for instruction librarians who want to learn how to create better research guides.

I mean *instruction librarians* in the broadest possible sense: that's any librarians who have a teaching role in their portfolio, and that can potentially include nearly any library staff members who interact with their library's public. At my library, most research guides are created by subject liaison librarians like myself (and I think that's true in most academic libraries), but also by our archivists, reference staff, scholarly communication librarian, instructional technology specialist, web services librarian, LIS interns, public services coordinators, and others.

By *better research guides*, I mean guides that serve as tools that our researchers will want to bookmark, use, return to, refer to, and most importantly learn from. With that last point firmly in mind, I've started from the assumption that at its best, a research guide isn't just a webpage, it's a teaching tool. I've taken some of the concepts from instructional theory and practice that have been most useful to me as a developing teacher over the years and tried to apply them to the question of how librarians can better use our research guides as a venue for teaching.

This raises some obvious questions. To name a few: How can a webpage teach? How do we know if students are actually using our guides? What do distance learners need from a guide that local users don't? How can we reach students with whom we never interact directly? In this book I'll try to answer those questions and others.

What Is Instructional Theory?

Instructional theory is simply theoretical background that helps teachers understand how students learn and how to improve our teaching. If you're a librarian who teaches, your work is already informed by instructional theory whether you realize it or not: any good practice that you've learned to use in your planning or in the classroom is probably based on instructional theory. I've considered how to apply teaching concepts like learning objectives, active learning, learning styles, assessment, and programmatic planning, as well as how to bring some basic principles of user experience to bear in designing guides. (We'll also look at some ideas that don't come from educational theory but from web designers.

Teaching is at the heart of the goal, but the medium in which we're working is web-based.)

In the coming chapters I'll examine how to use some ideas from teaching theory to create better research guides, such as these:

- *Learning objectives* (or learning outcomes) are simply statements that specify what students should be able to accomplish after a learning activity. Defining clear and specific learning objectives can help a guide's author keep focused on what students really need to know when using the guide.
- *Active learning* refers to learning by doing. Studies have shown that incorporating active elements into research guides can keep students engaged with a guide and encourage them to return to it throughout a class or research project.[1]
- *Learning styles* (or multiple intelligences) refers to the ways in which people approach learning differently: through text, visual elements, activities, and so on. Including different types of content in a guide can help a wider variety of learners understand your material. Learning styles are an important component of
- *Instructional design*, the practice of designing teaching materials to be more efficient, attractive, and effective to improve student learning. Instructional design has a great deal of influence on how students use guides. Instructional design includes concepts, like cognitive load theory, that describe how learners absorb information. It's related to the idea of
- *User experience*, a concept more usually associated with web design than with teaching. Since research guides exist as webpages, it's important for authors of research guides to understand how the experience of using a webpage has an impact on the learner.
- *Assessment* is an important element in teaching: gathering information about how well students have learned the desired material. We'll examine both how to use research guides as an assessment tool and how to assess guides for future improvement.
- *Programmatic planning* (or instructional program design) involves considering guides not only as discrete learning objects, but also in the broader context of other guides and the library's instructional plan as a whole.

Searching the LIS literature

I first became interested in library research guides as a topic of research a couple of years ago. When a colleague and I started looking for sources to inform a conference presentation we planned to give, we quickly discovered that searching the LIS databases for relevant articles was trickier than we expected.

I've settled on *research guide* as a standard term for the purposes of this book, but of course that is only one of many different descriptors used by librarians over the years. When the distinction matters, I sometimes refer to guides for a specific class as *course guides* and more general topic-based guides as *subject guides*, a distinction that seems logical to me even though many libraries seem to use *subject guides* as a descriptor for all their research guides. Not only have librarians used a wide range of terms to describe research guides in their writing, but also no standardized subject heading exists for these guides in the LIS databases I used while researching this book (*Library, Information Science & Technology Abstracts [LISTA]* and *Library and Information Science Abstracts [LISA]* among others).

A sampling of a few of the subject terms used for some of the relevant literature may suggest the challenge of researching this topic:

- Academic libraries—Computer network resources
- Computer network resources
- Computer-assisted instruction
- Internet
- Internet in education
- Internet instruction
- Online instruction
- Pathfinders
- Remote access networks
- Subject guides
- Tutorials
- User instruction
- Web sites
- Web-based instruction
- World wide web

Some of these are author-assigned keywords, some official subject headings, some (*Internet, computer network resources*) are so vague as to be useless, and no term that I could identify is applied to the topic with any consistency. Terms also change over time: *pathfinders* was once a more common term for *research guides* than it is today, and *tutorials* in an online context once referred to any webpage intended as a self-guided teaching tool but now is more likely to refer to a video learning object.

Again, this is just a sampling (and a set that I hand-picked to make a point, certainly not statistically representative), but it may illustrate the difficulty of doing a "perfect" literature search on research guides. Naturally, each chapter includes a bibliography to serve as a jumping-off point for your own research.

A Note about LibGuides

My own library creates our research guides using LibGuides, a product by the company Springshare. It's a content management system (or CMS: a system for creating and publishing webpages) designed specifically for librarians to use in creating online research guides, and I think it warrants a brief specific mention. LibGuides is so popular for its ease of use and simple, attractive design that *LibGuides* is on its way to becoming a near-synonym for *research guides*, and I wouldn't be at all surprised if within a few years the term has become the equivalent of *Band-Aid* or *Xerox* for librarians: a brand name so successful that it becomes genericized. (One 2011 study found that, of the 99 libraries surveyed, 67 were using LibGuides as their research guide platform.[2])

I'm a big fan of LibGuides, but this is emphatically not a LibGuides how-to book. All of the theory, principles, suggestions, examples, and ideas should be something that any instruction librarian can use with little or no trouble with any system or software. It doesn't matter if your library uses LibGuides, Library a la Carte, or Drupal; if you compose HTML in Notepad; or if you use a home-grown CMS that no one else has ever heard of. These ideas can work in many settings, no matter what specific technology tools you're using.

My Background

I've worked in libraries for about twenty years and have been teaching information literacy classes since 2001. My experience is entirely in academic libraries, and my writing may show a bias toward the academic library side of the profession. However, as I researched this book I made an effort to include examples from a variety of library types, and I believe that it will be useful to anyone creating guides in an instructional context, no matter who your audience is.

I've worked extensively with research guides for nearly ten years. As the LibGuides system administrator for two different academic libraries, I've had occasion to create and use a wide range of guides. I've also taught best practices for research guides in continuing education workshops.

My own research guides are located at research.library.gsu.edu. I don't claim that every guide I've created follows all the principles here, and some of my oldest guides don't even come close. In the last two to three years, I have become more consciously aware of the potential for improving research guides as teaching tools, I've thought more about *how* to do so, and in that time I've tried gradually to put more and more of these ideas into practice. Naturally, every guide, like every teacher, is always a work in progress.

Notes

1. Yunfei Du, "Exploring the Difference between 'Concrete' and 'Abstract,'" *Journal of Library & Information Services in Distance Learning* 1, no. 3 (September 2004): 53, 61, doi:10.1300/J192v01n03_04.
2. Jimmy Ghaphery and Erin White, "Library Use of Web-Based Research Guides," *Information Technology & Libraries* 31, no. 1 (March 2012): 22.

References

Du, Yunfei, "Exploring the Difference between 'Concrete' and 'Abstract,'" *Journal of Library & Information Services in Distance Learning* 1, no. 3 (September 2004): 53, 61, doi:10.1300/J192v01n03_04.

Ghaphery, Jimmy, and Erin White. "Library Use of Web-Based Research Guides." *Information Technology & Libraries* 31, no. 1 (March 2012): 21–31.

CHAPTER 1

Research Guides and Instructional Theory

What Is a Research Guide?

A RESEARCH GUIDE IS simply a webpage created by librarians for library users as an aid to their research. They're used widely by academic and school libraries, but also by public and special libraries and archives. Individual libraries may refer to these guides as subject guides, course guides, pathfinders, or other names depending on context, situation, or preference. (I'm mostly using *research guide* or simply *guide* for simplicity's sake in this book—sometimes *pathfinder* just for variety.)

Research guides are usually intended to address an audience with a particular and specific information need. They contain instructions, links, and other information meant to help users with a specific research context or task. Guides may exist to help library users complete a class assignment requiring research, accomplish a useful library procedure (placing an ILL request, checking out e-books), carry out research on a given topic or in a subject area, or perhaps learn to use a particular research tool like Zotero, Ancestry.com, or PsycINFO.

What Are Research Guides For?

Research guides are useful as a reference or instructional tool for library users who have a specific information need. They can serve a number of teaching-related functions.

One of the most common use cases for readers of this book is the course guide. This is a guide designed for students in a specific class, usually with a specific research assignment for which they need to use library information tools. Librarians design the course guide as a persistent resource, lasting beyond the class session, to provide information, research tools, and help specifically curated—and created—to address the research assignment.

Guides can serve as the equivalent of a paper handout in some ways. They give students a visual/textual document to reference during the instruction session, to reinforce and restate the instruction librarian's lecture and other live interactions. In some sense, they can function as an equivalent of written notes to make sure that the student has a record of all the information given in class, though with the possible disadvantage that the language of the guide isn't in the student's own words, as personal notes would be.

When designed with the class session in mind, a guide can work as an outline of the in-person class session, giving students a sense of where they are in the overall class plan—what's been covered already and what's to follow. For the instruction librarian, building the class outline into the course guide can do the same, helping to keep her on track during the session and possibly also obviating the need for written notes. Demonstrating to students that the librarian is using the same tool she recommends to them can reinforce its value as a research tool to be used after class.

Unlike the case with a paper handout or outline, students and the librarian can actually interact with the guide. Rather than asking students to consult a print handout for the name and description of a database, then locate it on the library site, having students work from a guide in class removes at least one step between them and the information resource they need: show them the link on the guide page, and they can get directly into it to search, which gets them to the hands-on search process more quickly. The librarian can even build specialized search tools like custom widgets directly into the guide.

Librarians can't reach every class and student with an instruction session. This may be due to too much demand for instruction or too many sections of a given class for the librarian to teach in person, disconnect between the teaching faculty and the library, or other reasons like simple student absence on the day of the library session. The research guide gives the librarian an easy means to provide at least some sort of instructional contact to potentially any student, even if their professor declined the offer of an instruction session or the student overslept that day. The guide can also refresh the memory of a student who did attend class but can't remember the name of that one really useful source for the research paper.

Most campuses also have some form of learning management system (LMS) like Blackboard Learn or Moodle, an online means of interaction with the course and the professor that students quickly become accustomed to using regularly. The research guide gives a subject librarian a relatively easy way to provide a library presence in the context of the course if the professor agrees to link or embed the guide into the class's LMS page.

Instruction librarians often suffer from insufficient classroom face time with students; we rarely have the opportunity to teach everything we'd wish to. Our total in-person contact with any given class may be limited to a single hour of the semester. This often requires some difficult choices about what to teach students and what to leave out. The research guide gives librarians a venue to provide some of the information that won't fit into the instruction session due to time constraints.

Chat-based online reference has become a popular service in many libraries. Research guides can be a useful supplement to chat reference: if the library has guides available that address common problems, it may be easier on both the reference librarian and the online patron to simply send a link to the relevant page of a guide. Having to spell out each step of a complex process—how to log into a library account, place an ILL request, renew books online, or other frequently asked questions—may sometimes be time-consuming and frustrating via the text-only medium of many chat reference services. Many library chat services lack a means of sharing screens or visually indicating points on a screen, so having some basic instructional guides prepared with screenshots and clear text instructions or brief tutorial videos can save repetitive explanations on the part of the librarian as well as more effectively clarifying a process for the online student. This works well with basic (but often multistep) procedures like those mentioned, but it can also be useful for more complex reference questions as well—some students may even be happier following instructions on a self-paced guide than having a librarian virtually hold their hand through a lengthy process.

Terminology Used in This Book

Research guide/pathfinder. Our working definition is above. When the context needs more specificity, I sometimes use *course guide* to refer to a guide designed for a specific class and *subject guide* for a guide to a broader topic such as an academic subject or similar area. I may use other variations that I hope will be clear from context. Although I called a research guide a webpage (singular) above, most guides are actually at least a few linked pages in size. While *research guide* or some variation is used by many libraries on their websites to describe this type of resource, *pathfinder* is jargon used by librarians among themselves but not when addressing users. In other words, we generally expect users to recognize *research guides* or similar terminology as a label on the library website, but not the term *pathfinder*.[1]

Librarian. Hopefully you know this term already, but note that I'm using the term *librarian* broadly and inclusively here to mean anyone who creates library research guides. In my experience in libraries, this has included not only professional librarians, but also reference and instruction paraprofessionals, instructional design staff, technology specialists, graduate assistants, and others.

Instructor/professor. Typically when I use the terms *instructor, professor,* or similar expressions, I'm referring to the instructor of record of a course: the student's regular teacher. Librarians do teach and are often faculty members, of course, but there are many occasions when I'll need to differentiate between a class's regular professor and the librarian supporting the class's research.

Students/users. Since I tackle this topic from the perspective of an academic librarian in a teaching role, most of the library users I personally deal with are students, and I will often refer to them as such. If you work in a different type of library, such as a public or special library, your guide users may not literally be students. Even if you're an academic librarian, a given research guide may not be aimed at a student audience—you may create guides intended for use by faculty, staff, or other constituencies. The teaching and design principles in this book will still help you improve your guides for any researchers or library users, whether or not they are literally students. Consider the terms *student, library user,* and *researcher* as interchangeable in most cases.

Assignment/information need. Again, my academic library experience often prompts me to speak of users' information needs in terms of classes and assignments. Even at a university library, there are many exceptions. Guide users often have learning needs not assigned by a professor: they may have a general-use need like catalog searching, a situational need like requesting an ILL item, or self-initiated needs like readers' advisory or job seeking. Feel free to translate *assignment* to *information need* if it makes more sense in your context. As long as you're thinking about what your user needs to learn from your guide and why, that's what matters.

Content management system/CMS/guide system/guide software/guide platform (and variants). These terms simply refer to whatever program or system your library uses to create your online research guides. *Content management system* (CMS) is a general term for any software used to publish web content. Many libraries have CMSs designed especially for creating research guides. These guide-specific platforms usually have features built in specifically for libraries' needs and may be designed for easier use by librarians who lack extensive web design experience. You may not have a separate or specialized CMS just for your research guides: many libraries use whatever software they already use to create their website.

At this writing, LibGuides by Springshare is probably the best-known of these specialized CMSs, but there are others like Library à la Carte and SubjectsPlus; other libraries use wikis or other platforms. This book is as "CMS-agnostic" as possible; it shouldn't matter what CMS you're using or whether you have a dedicated one just for creating guides. The principles and advice are applicable to any library's web environment. (Many of the examples do take the form of LibGuides, since so many libraries, including my own, use it.)

User experience/UX. User experience is a concept from web design (and other fields) concerned with how users feel when interacting with your site.[2] This sounds rather abstract, maybe even a bit too warm and fuzzy when phrased this way, but in fact a user's subjective perceptions and responses have a significant effect on how—and whether—they use your guide. UX combines pragmatic ideas of visual design, information architecture, and user behavior to inform how to make websites easier and more pleasant to use. Designing a guide with good UX in mind requires attention and care, but it isn't difficult. Chapter 4 talks much more about UX.

Common Problems in Creating Research Guides

A number of problems that often appear in research guides can make the guide more difficult to use or unattractive to the user. Chapter 4 includes advice for addressing these problems:

Too much information. Just as in planning instruction sessions, librarians often try to provide information in a guide to cover every possible contingency of a user's information needs. This causes comprehension problems when a student arrives at a guide needing help with a specific need and is presented with a bewildering array of options. This can be particularly true when the intended audience for a pathfinder is an inexperienced undergraduate student.

If the librarian has no clear starting point, defined progression through an assignment, or other plan for the structure of a new guide, the temptation is great to throw everything into the library's kitchen sink. Despite good intentions of attempting to provide everything the user *might* need, this approach confuses students and discourages them from using the overloaded guide. Instructional concepts like learning objectives and scaffolding and some simple user experience (UX) planning can help streamline guides to reduce the TMI problem.

Too much text. This is a special case of TMI that's worth examining a little more closely. It seems to be an occupational hazard that librarians are often highly textually oriented—when we wish to convey information, many of us tend to think in terms of writing large amounts of text rather than images or another medium that might convey equivalent information. No surprise there: we're a profession that's profoundly associated with textual information, so of course we're likely to be comfortable learning, teaching, and in general conveying ideas via text.

There's nothing wrong with using text in research guides, but too often we fail to take into account some important ideas: first, that our users may not be as text-oriented as we are, and second, that in general, the human eye takes in and processes text differently in a webpage on a screen than it does ink on a printed page. Most librarians don't learn how to write good, readable text *for the web* before we start creating guides. Editing (especially cutting down) and reformatting text on your guides can make a huge difference in how well your users understand the material you're presenting.

Poor visual design. Librarians (except web services librarians) also rarely get much training in good design principles and how design can have a positive or negative impact on how students are able to use and absorb information. Fortunately, most CMSs intended for creating research guides already provide an attractive, usable visual baseline as long as they aren't abused too badly with over-the-top images, colors, and fonts.

Nothing but links. Links to databases and other useful websites are common and necessary for most guides, but a guide that's nothing but a link farm doesn't convey a lot of information and isn't very useful as a teaching tool. A corollary to this problem is the guide that overwhelms the user with a long list of databases to choose from, but no guidance as to which ones might work best for a given type of research. This type of guide often annotates links only with text copied and pasted from the database vendor's description, full of jargon that goes over students' heads.

How Can Guides Teach?

Research guides have become one of the most frequently used tools in the instruction librarian's toolbox. We may use them as classroom teaching outlines, access points to library resources, sites for students to make contact with their liaison librarians, and even a replacement for in-person class sessions for online or absent students. Too often, though, what we call "guides" fail to live up to that name, consisting only of lists of links to databases with no real instructional content: "Given the importance and variety of goals assigned to research guides, it can … be striking how little time is devoted to questions of pedagogy and design."[3]

How can a web guide best live up to its potential use as an effective teaching tool? It doesn't have to be difficult, but, like a good classroom session, it does require the conscious application of good pedagogical concepts. Several concrete and practical ideas from instructional theory are particularly well suited to designing effective research guides. None of these require a deep or extensive pedagogical background to understand and apply: any librarian can easily learn to adapt these concepts to improve their guides.

Library instruction is most effective when directly tied to a course, and better yet to a specific assignment.[4] Students respond best to any form of instruction when they can see its direct benefit to their immediate information need. Designing a guide with students' assignment in mind, and building it around learning objectives taken from that assignment, makes it clear to students that the librarian understands and is addressing the work they have to do *right now*. It demonstrates the relevance and usefulness of the guide. Since guides are available 24/7, students can take advantage of them as learning opportunities in small bites, as needed, and at their own pace.

Good teaching also includes active learning activities and information in more than one medium, not just lectures.[5] What does this mean in the context of a web-based guide? Guide authors should take care not to present big chunks of "passive" information—long explanatory text can kill users' interest. A good guide can include active tools like search boxes, worked examples, and other interactive elements. Keep in mind that students learn best in a variety of ways: visually, textually, interactively, and even via other media like auditory elements.

Modeling good research practices and strategies can help students become aware of the skills involved in using library resources. Such modeling supports reflection during the research process and understanding of that process. This reflective situation, called metacognition ("thinking about thinking,") encourages students to think critically about the research itself, helping them generalize beyond the steps of the immediate research task to (hopefully) a deeper understanding of how to apply the skills to other assignments.[6] Structuring the guide around the learning objectives of the assignment supports metacognition as well, by "stepping back" from the close-up view of which databases to use, looking at the entire process, and breaking it into manageable pieces.

This breaking down of a larger topic, process, or task into smaller, more easily manageable, and less intimidating units is often called *chunking*.[7] Students have a finite capacity for how much material they can learn and process simultaneously. Learners must have the chance to absorb and understand incoming information in the short-term working memory before they can organize and store it in long-term memory, where it eventually becomes automatic without the need to consciously recall and analyze it, freeing up working memory again to learn new skills. By chunking information in a guide into digestible stages or pieces, the librarian avoids overwhelming students (causing "cognitive overload") and allows them to comfortably learn one objective before proceeding to the next.[8]

The best approach to organizing these instructional "chunks" is known as *scaffolding*: providing the user with all the needed information to accomplish the task or assignment, with appropriate guidance by an expert (librarian, in our case) available. Effectively scaffolded instruction is clear, is created with the user in mind, consists of carefully selected resources, models an appropriate path through the overall task, and—to keep students on track—is free of extraneous or distracting information.[9]

The ideas above are all adapted from best practices for classroom teaching. Most (but by no means all) librarians who create pathfinders have at least some experience with classroom instruction, and many of these ideas won't seem new, even if the instructor has never applied them to creating research guides.

Anyone who has taught a class understands that *how* information is presented to students can sometimes be nearly as important as the information itself. A class must be presented in a way that engages students' attention and interest, minimizes distractions from the topic at hand, and takes into account pragmatic environmental factors like how best to use the teaching space. The teacher makes choices (conscious or otherwise) about presentation methods, vocal delivery, and classroom management to give the students the best possible learning experience.

We make analogous choices in guide design for the same reasons. The information's container—in this case a webpage—has an effect on how the student experiences the instructional content, so it's important to understand how the presentation of factors like text, white space, visual elements, page length, and so on affect students' experience with a guide. This is where attention to UX has a positive effect on learning. To some extent, it's the web equivalent of classroom presentation skills. Like applying good classroom techniques to improve your teaching, it doesn't have to be difficult: learning or applying basic and effective techniques to make a guide an effective delivery system for your carefully crafted instructional material.

That's a brief outline of some of the key ways in which it's possible to take principles of good teaching, educational theory, and our understanding of how students learn, adapt the ideas to a web-based learning environment, and apply them to creating more effective library research guides. The rest of the book will consist of a deeper discussion of all these ideas (and some others) and examinations of how best to work with them in our context of library instruction.

Some of the ideas I'm discussing—web readability and comprehension, visual design, and UX—are not truly products of education theory, but they're relevant and useful here. The research guide is the teaching tool with which we're concerned, and these principles of online information use all apply directly to improving students' comprehension and absorption of your carefully designed instructional material.

Notes

1. Carla Dunsmore, "A Qualitative Study of Web-Mounted Pathfinders Created by Academic Business Libraries," *Libri: International Journal of Libraries & Information Services* 52, no. 3 (September 2002): 145. *Pathfinder* is a term that's mostly gradually fallen out of use in libraries, but I like the way the word sounds. I think it's vivid and descriptive even if it's not a term our users recognize. I gave an online talk about research guides in 2013 to the Southeastern New York Library Resources Council containing earlier versions of many of the ideas that appear in this book. Tessa Killian, who invited me to speak to the group, suggested "Modern Pathfinders" as the title of the presentation, and I liked it; it implies that we're giving an updated spin on an idea that's been around for a long time. With her permission I borrowed it for the title of this book.

2. Aaron Schmidt and Amanda Etches, *User Experience (UX) Design for Libraries* (Chicago: ALA TechSource, 2012), 1.

3. Caroline Sinkinson et al., "Guiding Design," *portal: Libraries & the Academy* 12, no. 1 (January 2012): 63.

4. Nancy H. Dewald, "Transporting Good Library Instruction Practices into the Web Environment," *Journal of Academic Librarianship* 25, no. 1 (January 1999): 26–31, doi:10.1016/S0099-1333(99)80172-4.

5. Ibid.

6. Veronica Bielat, Rebeca Befus, and Judith Arnold, "Integrating LibGuides into the Teaching-Learning Process," in *Using LibGuides to Enhance Library Services*, ed. Aaron W. Dobbs, Ryan L. Sittler, and Douglas Cook (Chicago: ALA TechSource, 2013), 125.

7. Ibid., 123.

8. Jennifer J. Little, "Cognitive Load Theory and Library Research Guides," *Internet Reference Services Quarterly* 15, no. 1 (2010): 54–55.

9. Bielat, Befus, and Arnold, "Integrating LibGuides," 123–24.

References

Bielat, Veronica, Rebeca Befus, and Judith Arnold. "Integrating LibGuides into the Teaching-Learning Process." In *Using LibGuides to Enhance Library Services: A LITA Guide*, edited by Aaron W. Dobbs, Ryan L. Sittler, and Douglas Cook, 121–42. Chicago: ALA TechSource, an imprint of the American Library Association, 2013.

Dewald, Nancy H. "Transporting Good Library Instruction Practices into the Web Environment: An Analysis of Online Tutorials." *Journal of Academic Librarianship* 25, no. 1 (January 1999): 26–31. doi:10.1016/S0099-1333(99)80172-4.

Dunsmore, Carla. "A Qualitative Study of Web-Mounted Pathfinders Created by Academic Business Libraries." *Libri: International Journal of Libraries & Information Services* 52, no. 3 (September 2002): 137–56.

Little, Jennifer J. "Cognitive Load Theory and Library Research Guides." *Internet Reference Services Quarterly* 15, no. 1 (2010): 53–63.

Schmidt, Aaron, and Amanda Etches. *User Experience (UX) Design for Libraries.* Chicago: ALA TechSource, an imprint of the American Library Association, 2012.

Sinkinson, Caroline, Stephanie Alexander, Alison Hicks, and Meredith Kahn. "Guiding Design: Exposing Librarian and Student Mental Models of Research Guides." *portal: Libraries & the Academy* 12, no. 1 (January 2012): 63–84.

CHAPTER 2

Learning Objectives in Research Guides

INSTRUCTION LIBRARIANS OFTEN HAVE strictly limited face-to-face time with students. The one-shot, one-hour classroom session is the staple of our teaching environment. As a result, we're constantly tempted to throw too much information into any teaching situation: after all, we may never have the chance to talk to these students again. If this is the only library class they're going to get, we'd better show them everything useful we can think of. Right?

It's more likely that students would benefit from a class session less jam-packed with information. Rather than teaching them "how to use the library" in an hour, show them the three or four tasks they need to accomplish their immediate research need. If this assignment calls for scholarly articles, teach them how to search for, identify, and obtain those, and skip the call number discussion. If they need historic newspapers or election poll data, don't bother showing them how to renew books online, even if it will probably come in handy for them to know that. (Hopefully that information exists elsewhere on your library's site.)

This idea—determining what specific tasks or skills students should be able to achieve and focusing the class on just those outcomes—is not a revelation to experienced instruction librarians. In fact, when stated like this, it can seem ridiculously obvious. But the problem of trying to fit too much information into a class session—and more to the point here, into a research guide—really does plague many information literacy teachers. In a face-to-face class, it leaves many bored and confused students wondering "Why do I need to know this?" On a research guide, students won't stick around to be confused for more than a few seconds. If they don't see what they need quickly, they will simply click away and look elsewhere for something more obviously useful to their assignment.

The solution to this problem lies in thinking like a student, understanding what they need from the library in this specific class, putting yourself into their shoes as a researcher, and organizing your instructional tools—including research guides in particular—based on this insight and understanding. In short, a little thoughtful planning goes a long way.

The same approach that helps keep class sessions useful and interesting for students can make research guides more relevant and engaging: analyze what students need for *this* assignment (or task, or other information-seeking situation), eliminate anything not relevant, and break it down into clear and manageable parts. I recommend two simple and straightforward ideas to help plan and organize research guides, improve the focus of your guides to improve student learning, and avoid overloading students with irrelevant information.

First, *creating learning objectives* based on the students' assignment or other information need will not only aid your guide planning, but will also help you provide students with information that is clearly relevant to their need.

A second technique that follows naturally is organizing the material on your guides in accord with the research process—breaking it into smaller discrete stages that build on one another. This idea is called *chunking*, dividing information into smaller units that students can digest more easily.

We'll discuss the idea of chunking in a bit more detail below, and again in chapter 4's discussion of user experience design, but for now bear in mind that in the context of online research guides it's particularly important to break up teaching material into smaller segments. The human eye and brain take in information on a webpage differently from information on a printed page, and providing too much content on a single page of a research guide can overwhelm students' ability to absorb the material.

What Is a Learning Objective?

Spending some time before planning a class figuring out students' specific information needs—or learning objectives—can make all the difference in students' experience during a class session: their motivation to learn, their attention to the material, and the effectiveness of their learning.

That's a simple and fundamental idea from in-person teaching that can help an instructor design any sort of teaching tool or event, including web-based research guides. In the same way that we plan a class session's objectives, giving some thought to clarifying learning objectives before starting work on a research guide can make it much easier for students to find and retain the information they need.

Many works on library instruction feature discussion of learning objectives in much more detail than I will go into here—but let's start with a brief explanation of what they are and how to create them as you plan your research guide.

Stated simply, a learning objective specifies a single task, function, or operation that students should be able to successfully accomplish after taking part in a learning activity.[1] Often that learning activity is attending a class, but of course there may be many other contexts, such as viewing a tutorial or, as we're discussing here, using an online research guide.

Typical learning objectives for a library class or research guide could include

- After reading the course guide, students will be able to search Academic Search Complete using appropriate subject keywords.
- By completing the exercises, students will create a journal article citation in APA style.
- At the conclusion of the tutorial, users will be able to download and install Zotero on their computers.

Defining Your Learning Objectives

To define a learning objective, just take a moment to think about what students probably cannot do before using the guide that they need to be able to do in order to accomplish their assignment. It sounds ridiculously simple—and it can be—but omitting this planning stage can result in a research guide that's vague, less engaging and less useful. In fact, consider explicitly spelling out the learning objectives on the first page of your guide (figure 2.1)—it can be a clear way to express to students exactly what they need to know and to demonstrate that the guide they're looking at is specifically relevant to the assignment they're working on.

ENGL 110 Learning Objectives: Library Instruction

After taking the ENGL 110 Library Instruction class, you should be able to do the following:

1. Given a broad research topic, use the 4W questions (who, what, where, when) to write a research question.
2. Given a research topic, pick out the key concepts and compile a list of search terms or keywords.
3. Given background information about Google and the Library, list two differences between information found on Google versus through the Library related to content, organization, quality or access.
4. Given a research topic and access to the library's catalog, find one relevant book on your topic and record all relevant citation information.
5. Given a research topic and access to a general article index database, find one relevant article on your topic and record all relevant citation information.

FIGURE 2.1

These learning objectives appear on a first-year English guide at Loyola Marymount University. This same language could be used by the librarian to plan an instruction session or to clarify to students the aims of this guide.

In the same way, including those same objectives on a slide at the beginning of a live instruction session can help give the library instructor credibility with students by demonstrating to them that the librarian actually understands their assignment and is going to address their specific information needs during the class session. Think of it as a way to show students that they've come to the right place as well as a way to focus your own instructional planning.

Most instruction librarians don't design research guides or class sessions in a vacuum; we come in as a guest instructor for a regular faculty member who teaches the course. Typically, students' information need comes from an assignment given by the regular professor. If the librarian hopes to create a useful and effective research guide, it's crucial for her to communicate with the professor giving the assignment. Ideally, this includes

- *Getting a copy of the actual assignment as given to the student.*
  An e-mail or description of the assignment from the professor is often a poor substitute: the teacher may forget to mention details

like types of required sources, length, due dates, topic requirements, or other parameters. Having an actual copy of the same
assignment that the student will be consulting is extremely helpful when trying to put yourself into the student's shoes to think
through the steps of the research process.

— If there is no assignment, as in the case of a more general
subject guide (figure 2.2) or a guide that teaches some
non-course-specific task such as creating bibliographies
or writing literature reviews, outline for yourself (on paper, or at least mentally) what the learner will need to be
able to accomplish. It might even be *more* important to
define the objectives of a non-course-based guide since
there's no external assignment to give it context.

General Nursing Research Guide by Southern Connecticut State University

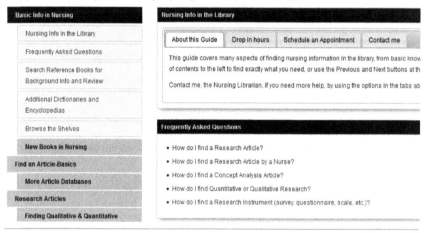

FIGURE 2.2

This general nursing research guide by Southern Connecticut State
University (http://libguides.southernct.edu/nursing) isn't focused
on a specific assignment but still puts learning objectives front and
center. The FAQ section on the first page directs students to relevant
parts of the guide using language they're likely to recognize from their
classwork.

- *Sharing your planned learning objectives with the professor.* Once you've sketched out what you see as the key learning objectives for the research guide and library class, run them by the course instructor and make sure you're covering the essentials. Often you'll find that you've thought of some things the instructor hasn't or that they've failed to mention something they want you to make sure to cover. This is a great way to get feedback on your instructional planning.
- *Sending the guide to the professor before sharing it with students.* This allows you both to make sure you've included any specific resources, instructions, and sources that the professor wants students to use and gives you both a chance to make sure you're on the same page—doubly important if you will be teaching a live class along with providing a research guide.
- *Encouraging the professor to share the guide with students.* The syllabus and the school's online course management system are both good places to expose students to the research guide. The teacher may be willing to e-mail your guide to the class before the library session if a live class is planned. If students can (or are required to) review your guide before class, it gives them a preview of what kind of research they'll be doing and may encourage them to think about questions to bring with them to the library session. It can even result in very ambitious or motivated students reaching out to you for consultation requests on their own initiative.

While we want students to learn as much as possible about research and the library, bear in mind that this guide, and this class, will not (we hope) be their one and only exposure to the library and library instruction. It is one of many opportunities the student will have to engage with the library, learning a little more each time.

Just as students learn, say, chemistry in small increments by engaging in specific experiments, they learn library research skills by engaging in specific research tasks. Cover just what they need and no more. Undergrads are used to learning management systems (LMSs) like Blackboard Learn, Moodle, or Angel, in which each of their classes has a specific page or site devoted to it—so this model makes sense to them in the context of library guides as well.[2]

Example: From Assignment to Objectives

A senior-level undergraduate speech and rhetoric course has the following assignment:

> Identify and define a group or culture unlike themselves to focus on the relationship between diversity and communication. The final paper will consist of an identification essay detailing this group's identity and culture, a literature review using scholarly journal articles that examine the group's communication practices, and an examination of media representations of this group (in film, news, television or other public media). The finished paper will include a bibliography in APA style.

The librarian defines major learning objectives based on this assignment. Two major ones jump out clearly. Students definitely need to be able to

- locate journal articles in library databases relevant to their group's communication practices
- locate media representations of their group in news, visual, or other media

The librarian could also include some or all of the following as objectives. Students should be able to

- locate sources defining and describing their group
- write a literature review
- cite sources in APA style

There could be others, of course, and many of these could be broken down into sub-objectives like *search the library catalog, distinguish scholarly articles from popular ones, define the purpose of a literature review,* and so on, but this is a high-level plan aimed at identifying only the major objectives. Detail can come later.

continued on next page···

··· **Example (continued)**

She decides to use the first two major objectives for sure. Based on her experience with senior classes and this professor, they should already have had some experience identifying what makes a scholarly article, but they will need recommended databases and search strategies for this specific topic. They will also need help searching for news sources and film and television, as that's a somewhat less common research task and may take some creative thinking depending on the students' chosen groups.

She considers *write a literature review* as important enough to include as a third objective for the guide. Many undergraduates will not have experience at this task, and a page defining the role and purpose of a lit review, and how to approach the necessary library research, will help reinforce whatever discussion the professor plans to have in class about lit reviews.

Sources defining the group may be a moot point by the time the students encounter the guide, but she can still include some recommendations in a sidebar. A link or page about APA style and citation software is always useful to include, but won't be the major focus to this particular guide.

Library users are likely consulting your guide because they have a specific and immediate research need. Don't overwhelm them with too much information. Don't confuse them by providing information irrelevant to their present task. This is important not only for novice undergraduate researchers, but for graduate students as well: experienced researchers often have very specific discipline-based information needs.[3]

Thinking specifically and consciously about learning objectives may be the single practice that has most improved my library instruction: it causes me to think in terms of what information the students actually *need* right now, not what *I* think they should know in the long term. It shows that the librarian understands the work that they're doing and builds their confidence in the library as a source of credible, relevant expert advice.

Actually writing out learning objectives may sound like elementary busy work, but it really is a valuable planning step: it focuses the guide author's attention on the assignment, encourages her to think like a student and mentally step through what the student actually needs to accomplish by using the library, and creates at least a rough outline of the key material to include in the guide. It not only clarifies the instructional plan in the librarian's mind, but also gives students an overview of what skills and processes are needed to succeed at the assignment.[4] Verbalizing the objectives in a concrete form gives them helpful specificity: "Students need to be able to locate books in the catalog on their chosen nineteenth-century US president" is much more descriptive and leads to more precise teaching ideas than "I should include a section on catalog searching."

Learning objectives are typically expressed by assembling a few parts: the *stem*, the *action verb*, and the *outcome*.[5]

The Stem

The stem is the simplest part. It simply defines the context in which the learning takes place. For example:

- After consulting the research guide, students will be able to …
- At the completion of the class, learners will …
- By working through the provided exercises, the student will do …

This is really the least crucial part of the objective; it's often the same for all objectives and can often be repeated or sometimes even left implicit.

The Action Verb

The verb requires more thought. What do students need *to be able to do*? This is really the linchpin of the learning objective. Once you've taught them how to do something, or explained a concept, or demonstrated a task, what will they be able to do that they couldn't before? Examples of action verbs in an objective could include

- search
- locate
- define
- distinguish
- identify
- cite

… or of course many others.

When selecting verbs for learning outcomes, look at the assignment, talk to the course instructor, and above all think through the information needs and processes from the learner's perspective. If they have to write a paper, they may need to *select* a relevant database search tool, *search for* or *locate* sources, *distinguish* primary from secondary sources, *select* useful sources based on subject headings, and *cite* sources in a given style.

It's often tempting to use *understand* as the verb in a learning objective—that's the bottom line of what we want our students to do, right? They should *understand* all the stuff we're teaching them!—but avoid using this verb in your objectives.

The verbs in your learning objectives should ideally be *observable* or *assessable* in some way. Even if, as is often the case in the context of a research guide, you won't *actually* be observing students during the learning process or at work afterwards, thinking in terms of observable skills or tasks helps clarify the activities students will need to undertake. *Understand* and its synonyms are not easy to observe and don't involve the student doing anything active. Think like a student again: from their point of view, their ultimate goal (let's be brutally frank here) isn't necessarily to understand—it's to accomplish a task and turn in a research assignment.

Understanding comes through doing. *Understanding* the difference between primary and secondary sources isn't *doing* anything—but you could hypothetically ask a student to demonstrate that they can *identify* or *distinguish* one from the other by selecting them from search results. It may seem like a minor distinction, but it can bring clarity to your planning and teaching.

The Outcome

Finally, flesh out the action verb by adding an ultimate outcome. The outcome is simply the result of the action. What is it your learners need to be able to define, search, compare, use, or describe? Like the stem, this gives context, but the context is about the students' information need.

We've already looked at several possibilities for outcomes above, and if you have a good grasp of the assignment, then these too should take little extra preparation: students may need to identify *primary sources*, or cite *journal articles*, or locate *nineteenth-century biographies*, or read *call numbers*. It's also fine to add more detail to clarify how or why these things are essential to meeting the information need. This often (but not always) includes the phrase *in order to* or something similar. Remember to keep it specific: "… read call numbers in order to locate useful sections of the library stacks for topic browsing," for example.

Some completed learning objectives might look like these:

- After reading the research guide, students will be able to locate relevant subject encyclopedias in order to identify potential research topics.
- After using the guide, participants will be able to identify the parts of a citation in MLA style in order to read a bibliography.
- After working through the activity, learners will be able to identify peer-reviewed academic sources relevant to their topic.

Whenever possible, *use the same language* in your objectives that the instructor uses in the assignment itself. If the professor refers to parts of an assignment as a "case study" and a "scholarly analysis," reiterate those exact terms in your learning objectives and use that language throughout your guide: "This page includes resources to *find newspaper articles for the case study portion of your assignment*," for example.

This is important! It helps students recognize that they are on the right track when they see that the library guide offers guidance using the same terminology that their professor uses in class and on their syllabus. Pay attention to whether the assignment directs students to find "peer-reviewed articles" or "scholarly sources," to create a "bibliography" or a "works cited list," to find "journalistic treatments" or "news coverage." While librarians may be able to recognize these as synonyms, an inexperienced student may not and may just be skimming your guide looking for terms he recognizes from class.

The flip side of this argument is that students *will* need to learn a certain number of terms and vocabulary that are specific to their major discipline and to library research. Shouldn't we be using that terminology in our guides? To some extent, absolutely yes, but meet them halfway to make sure they can follow you instead of becoming lost. Make sure you're distinguishing in your own mind between terms students may need to learn to navigate the research process (*peer-reviewed, catalog, interlibrary loan*) and terms that are either LIS-specific jargon or so vague as to be unhelpful (*records* as in catalog or database records, *items, resources, holdings*).

Undergraduate researchers in particular are often unclear about what types of resources they need to accomplish a research assignment. Their lack of confidence can lead to confusion and library anxiety.[6] One strength of a well-designed research guide is the ease with which even novice researchers recognize its applicability to the specifics of their assignment: "For instance, the headings of analyst reports or company rankings should make perfect sense to a business student, but they are not library-lingo and do not present the information sources in terms that a librarian would understand, such as 'bibliographies' and 'indexes and abstracts.'"[7]

"Chunking"

The human brain can take in only a limited amount of information at once. Good teachers quickly learn not to overwhelm students by giving them too much, breaking up material into discrete units to be absorbed one by one. This idea goes by the inelegant term *chunking*—dividing up learning into manageable bites to better fit the brain's capacity for short-term memory and learning.

In order for real learning to take place, information is processed in short-term, or working, memory, and passed into long-term memory as it is understood.[8] Cognitive capacity for learning is finite, and students can become lost if too much information is presented to them at one time: it overwhelms the short-term capacity and is never absorbed into long-term memory where it can be used. Chunking the material decreases the load on the brain and allows for learning to take place more easily.

It's an easy idea to adapt into research guide design. Each chunk—typically equivalent to one learning objective—becomes a discrete unit of content on the guide. In most cases, one chunk can translate into a single page or section of the guide. Ideally, as we'll see in a later chapter, each chunk should consist of about enough information to fit on a typical web browser screen without the user needing to scroll down. Web design and user experience experts have established that readers are less likely to absorb information located below the first screen of material.[9]

Guides that are clearly chunked into learning objectives also provide easy navigation among sections and topics, allowing students to choose what parts of the guide to use and in what order. This is an important distinction from (and in some ways perhaps advantage over) in-class instruction: the medium of hypertext was *created* to allow the user to choose his

own information pathway, as opposed to the instruction session which follows the instructor's plan.[10]

Putting Objectives to Work in Your Research Guides

Once you've worked out the needed learning objectives, the next step is
to apply them the structure of the research guide. Putting some thought
and planning into learning objectives is an effective way to get away from
thinking like a librarian and getting closer to seeing the research task from
the learner's perspective. It does not have to be a time-consuming process,
but it does require some conscious thought on the librarian's part from the
outset.

One of the most common ways to organize a research guide is by format of material: a page of links and instructions labeled "Books" with guidance for using the catalog, a page labeled "Articles" with database links,
perhaps a page labeled "Websites" with links to materials available on the
open Web, and even a separate page of "Reference Works" with recommendations for how to locate materials in the reference stacks.

This is a natural way for the librarian brain to organize a guide. We
treat sources differently based on their type every day: serials are cataloged,
shelved, and circulated differently from monographs, reference books from
stacks books, microfilm from print and audiovisual material, and electronic resources differently from physical ones.

Many library websites, not just guides, are very strongly organized
around format of information since we have to access different formats by
using different tools or by going to different locations in the building. This
practice needs to change. Guides give us the chance to offer users an alternative path to information that makes more sense to them.

Users tend to prefer, and better understand, guides organized around
their research needs rather than information format (figure 2.3).[11] Students
see library resources differently from their side of the equation: all these
resources are a means to an end, and in many cases it doesn't matter to
them what physical or electronic form the information takes, as long as it
fills the requirements of the assignment. This may be especially true in the
context of an online guide, where the physical setting of the library is much
less relevant to finding the information.

Social Work Guide

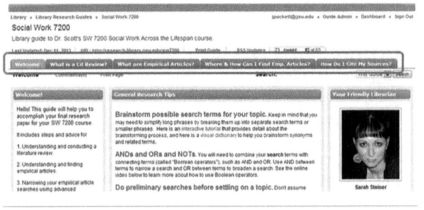

FIGURE 2.3

This guide by Sarah Steiner at Georgia State University is chunked into learning objectives using clear language based on the students' assignment.

Organize by what the student needs. For example, historically, the library catalog figured prominently in paper-based pathfinders, but it shows up less centrally in many web-based guides. To a librarian the catalog may be a vital tool in many contexts, but it could be irrelevant to a student requiring extremely current information and data for a business assignment.[12]

Kill the "Welcome" Page

Many librarians start their guides off with a welcome page—a homepage that gives the name of the relevant course, some general research tips, contact information for the library or librarian, and so on.

I suggest avoiding starting guides with this type of page. While all of this information is indeed helpful for the student to know, remember that students will be quickly skimming the page at first to see if it's relevant to their immediate information need.

Kill the "Welcome" Page (continued)···

··· **Kill the "Welcome" Page (continued)**

The best way to capture the attention of a student in this mode is to start the guide off with content that directly addresses one of the learning objectives. A page that asks and answers the question "How do you find articles for your annotated bibliography assignment?" in so many words has much clearer utility and interest for a student doing research than one labeled "Welcome" that buries your carefully crafted instructions and help behind a link or on the second page.

Don't be afraid to delete the welcome page and go straight for the how-to. Your users are unlikely to miss it.

Learning objectives help us think like a student and construct guides that better reflect how they approach their research. By taking those objectives and building guides around them, the librarian

- Creates guides that are more readily identified and understood by student researchers. Many students fail to match existing library guides with their information needs.[13] Tailoring the guide as specifically as possible to the steps of the research process—the learning objectives—encourages students to make use of the guide and helps them understand what it's for.
- Maps out a series of stages that helps students see research as a multistep process. Many students inexperienced with research assignments may see "library searching" as a single monolithic operation, and subdividing the research for an assignment may introduce them to the idea that different parts of an assignment call for different techniques.
  - Librarians find that this multistage approach helps students understand the process better. In one study of guides created for a business course, for example, "The industry guide broke down the information resources according to a step-wise and logical pattern. First the student needed overview information to understand the industry, next they needed to reference a standard industrial classification scheme, and then to refer to government information that utilized the SIC code."[14]

- Aligns the guide directly with the assignment or other course content. By providing students with a guide based directly on their assignment, she reinforces the idea that the research itself is an integral part of the assignment.
- Provides scaffolding for student learning. When an assignment is broken into multiple objectives, each objective can build on the previous knowledge, helping prevent students from becoming overloaded with too much information all at once (see the section on "chunking" above).

Example: Planning a Guide from Objectives

In the previous example, the librarian decided on three objectives for the research guide:

- locate journal articles relevant to their group's communication practices
- locate media representations of their group in news, visual, or other media
- write a literature review of research done on this group's communication practices

Assuming she's using LibGuides, these will probably be the first three tabs or pages on the guide; in a different guide CMS, they might be laid out some other way, but should be the three main visible "chunks" around which the guide is organized. She decides to order the pages to fit the likely sequence of students' work in the assignment:

- *Literature review sources.* This page will include recommended databases and search strategies.
- *Writing lit reviews.* This page will include information about the role and structure of the literature review in a research paper.
- *Media representations.* This page will include recommended sources for news articles and other media about the chosen group.

She chooses the page titles to match the language the professor uses in the assignment: "media representations" and not "news sources" or "media portrayals" to help students recognize which pages match which elements of the assignment.

Building a Guide Structure from Your Objectives

With all these principles in mind, an initial plan for the research guide falls neatly into place:

- Strategize before you start creating your guide.
- Consult the assignment, if there is one—or if there's not, sketch out an outline of your understanding of the tasks students need to accomplish to satisfy their information need.
- Develop learning objectives based on this need. Be specific. No single guide can teach "how to use the library." Don't try. Focus on this task, this class, this assignment, and eliminate irrelevant information.
- Signal the topics of the page—the chunked content—with clear headings to help students understand the overall organization of the guide. Clear labels with familiar language can make the difference between a researcher using the guide or passing it over entirely.[15]

As always, remember that while all of these guidelines are based on sound instructional principles, there will be many cases in which your own experience as a teacher, knowledge of your library's constituency, and other circumstances may trump this plan. Be prepared to be flexible and creative: these are best practices, not unbreakable rules.

Now the plan is in place for *what* the guide should teach. The next chapter will look at some ideas to help decide *how* best to approach teaching via a research guide, and how best to reach your students in this format.

Notes

1. Some authors distinguish sharply between learning "objectives" (what the teacher intends to cover in class or in a guide) and learning "outcomes" (what the student should be able to accomplish after learning). I don't find the distinction critical in this context as long as the core idea is understood: the instructor defines, to an appropriate degree of specificity, what students need to learn in a given situation. I usually use *objective*, but I sometimes use *outcome* more or less interchangeably.
2. Brenda Reeb and Susan Gibbons, "Students, Librarians, and Subject Guides," *portal: Libraries & the Academy* 4, no. 1 (January 2004): 126.

3. Caroline Sinkinson et al., "Guiding Design," *portal: Libraries & the Academy* 12, no. 1 (January 2012): 77.
4. Nancy H. Dewald, "Transporting Good Library Instruction Practices into the Web Environment," *Journal of Academic Librarianship* 24, no. 1 (January 1999): 26–27, doi:10.1016/S0099-1333(99)80172-4.
5. For a good crash-course summary, look at "Learning Objectives: Stems and Samples," Education Oasis, 2004, http://www.educationoasis.com/instruction/bt/learning_objectives.htm.
6. Sinkinson et al., "Guiding Design," 77.
7. Carla Dunsmore, "A Qualitative Study of Web-Mounted Pathfinders Created by Academic Business Libraries," *Libri: International Journal of Libraries & Information Services* 52, no. 3 (September 2002): 147.
8. Jennifer J. Little, "Cognitive Load Theory and Library Research Guides," *Internet Reference Services Quarterly* 15, no. 1 (2010): 54.
9. Jakob Nielsen, "F-Shaped Pattern for Reading Web Content," Nielsen Norman Group, April 17, 2006, http://www.nngroup.com/articles/f-shaped-pattern-reading-web-content.
10. Dewald, "Transporting Good Library Instruction Practices," 30.
11. Sinkinson et al., "Guiding Design," 73–74.
12. Dunsmore, "A Qualitative Study of Web-Mounted Pathfinders," 149.
13. Reeb and Gibbons, "Students, Librarians, and Subject Guides," 124.
14. Dunsmore, "A Qualitative Study of Web-Mounted Pathfinders," 148.
15. W. J. Jackson, "The User-Friendly Library Guide," *College & Research Libraries News* 45, no. 9 (1984): 470.

References

Dewald, Nancy H. "Transporting Good Library Instruction Practices into the Web Environment: An Analysis of Online Tutorials." *Journal of Academic Librarianship* 25, no. 1 (January 1999): 26–31. doi:10.1016/S0099-1333(99)80172-4.

Dunsmore, Carla. "A Qualitative Study of Web-Mounted Pathfinders Created by Academic Business Libraries." *Libri: International Journal of Libraries & Information Services* 52, no. 3 (September 2002): 137–56.

Education Oasis. "Learning Objectives: Stems and Samples," 2004. http://www.educationoasis.com/instruction/bt/learning_objectives.htm.

Jackson, W. J. "The User-Friendly Library Guide." *College & Research Libraries News* 45, no. 9 (1984): 468–71.

Little, Jennifer J. "Cognitive Load Theory and Library Research Guides." *Internet Reference Services Quarterly* 15, no. 1 (2010): 53–63.

Nielsen, Jakob. "F-Shaped Pattern for Reading Web Content." Nielsen Norman Group, April 17, 2006. http://www.nngroup.com/articles/f-shaped-pattern-reading-web-content.

Reeb, Brenda, and Susan Gibbons. "Students, Librarians, and Subject Guides: Improving a Poor Rate of Return." *portal : Libraries & the Academy* 4, no. 1 (January 2004): 123–30.

Sinkinson, Caroline, Stephanie Alexander, Alison Hicks, and Meredith Kahn. "Guiding Design: Exposing Librarian and Student Mental Models of Research Guides." *portal: Libraries & the Academy* 12, no. 1 (January 2012): 63–84.

CHAPTER 3

Learning Styles

Introduction

THERE ARE (AT LEAST) two broad strategies for making guides more approachable and useful for students. The first is pedagogical in nature: target the contents and organization of a guide to best address the information needs of your users, as discussed in the previous chapter and several to follow. The second is design-based: use principles of web usability to design the guide to fit in with how students are likely to read and work with your pages.

In a sense, the idea of learning styles—individual aptitudes or preferences for learning and processing information in different ways—overlaps both of these broad strategies, by connecting pedagogical ideas to those of web design. Not only must the material in a guide be created with an understanding of students' information needs in a specific situation, but ideally it should also be composed and presented with an eye toward the different ways in which students take in and process information.

Learning styles represent a theory that can help improve our understanding of student learning. Much of the literature about learning styles, both in the LIS instruction context and from other areas of education, is written from the classroom teaching perspective. Learning styles can be particularly useful in the context of the online teaching environment, however, because the web gives us the opportunity to present information in a wide variety of styles. Too often librarians fail to take advantage of the medium to improve their online guides. The medium of web-based guides is well suited to certain styles of information, such as visual and textual, but other approaches can be applied as well. Ideas from classroom instruction can either be directly adapted to the web medium or can at least help us understand students' learning strengths and weaknesses in order to make them more comfortable with the material we present and encourage them to use our guides more and to learn more from our guides.

This chapter explains what learning styles are and examines a few representative models of learning styles and a few critiques of the styles concept. We'll then move on to some practical applications and ideas for how learning style theory can be used to help inform our approach to research guide design, with a few potential problems and thoughts about best practices.

What Are Learning Styles?

Learning styles is a term used to describe the idea that learners may perceive, interact with, and respond to information more effectively when that information is presented in different ways—such as textual, auditory, visual, interactive, and so on—and that individual learners may have an optimal or preferred style of learning. Researchers in the field of education define the concept differently from one another, resulting in different ways of describing or modeling learning styles, but the idea centers around the theory that individuals learn best through a specific sense or particular type of experience.[1]

Synonyms and related concepts include *intellectual styles, learning preferences, cognitive styles, learning modalities, multiple intelligences,* and other terms that are often used interchangeably.[2] (I'll mostly continue to use *learning styles* for consistency, but the bibliography of this chapter shows that many other terms are used in the literature. "Cognitive styles" may be a useful LC subject heading for those doing research on the topic.) The earliest scholarly works on learning styles date back to the 1960s (or arguably 1950s) and came to real attention by the 1970s, and the idea that different students relate better to different approaches has remained a widely used concept in education since then.

Learning style does not indicate ability or intelligence. It is a preference, not even necessarily a conscious one, for expressing or using abilities in a particular way. We often talk about style preferences in absolute terms:

visual learners or kinesthetic learners and so on. Naturally, real-world individuals typically reflect a *mixture* of learning styles, and it would be rare to find someone who occupied the extreme end of any given scale. Educational scholars indicate that individual learning styles may be influenced by such factors as culture, gender, age, and of course individual personality and preference,[3] but the important takeaway for instruction librarians is simply that individual students may take to learning more readily when information is presented in one of their preferred styles.

Librarians on culturally diverse campuses may need to pay particular attention to creating guides with a variety of learning styles in mind. Many researchers conclude that students' culture of origin plays a significant role in style preference: for example, they find that Native North Americans and Latinos may prefer cooperative and interactive learning, often with more visual context; European Americans may prefer more individual learning; African Americans may prefer less structured learning experiences; and Asian Americans favor more structured activities with reflection time built in.[4]

Racial and other groupings like these are certainly generalizations (and ones that I take with a grain of salt), but think of this example as a reminder that different populations may need specialized attention to their learning style preferences. You probably know best whether your constituency, or your audience for a particular research guide, includes significant representation from particular populations. Does your public library serve a neighborhood with many residents whose first language is not English? If so, what do you know about their communication preferences—are they more comfortable with written language than spoken? Do you liaise with an academic department whose students might be trained to prefer a particular style? (For example: literature students may logically respond well to textual information, and art history students to images.) Is a guide intended for a freshman learning community oriented toward a particular field of study? Or, looking at the question from the other side, is the students' assignment or the subject matter of your guide particularly well suited to a specific style like visual illustrations or active exercises?

Before we look at some learning style theories, bear in mind that while it may be tempting to classify learners as solely preferring a particular style, in reality most people don't fit neatly into a single box. Students do not learn the same way in all situations, nor do most people *only* learn well in a particular style. Most learners are multimodal and multisituational, adapting their learning strategy to fit the present context as needed.[5] Using multiple learning styles can help reinforce ideas for students and can clarify ambiguous material by representing it in different ways, but no single style will be the perfectly "right" one for any audience or context.

In fact, educators and researchers often argue that the best approach is *not* to attempt to perfectly adapt class material to the student's preferred learning style. Doing so can actually have drawbacks: it could reinforce a student's learning preference to the point that she has difficulty learning in other ways or limit her problem-solving skills in contexts outside the controlled educational environment.[6] Shifting among different learning style strengths also helps students process the material and absorb it from short-term memory to long-term learning. Encountering information in a variety of formats—visual, abstract, textual, and so on—requires students to exercise a variety of perceptual strengths, and processing it in these different formats stimulates different mental focuses and helps students achieve better learning.[7]

The best approach may be to present material in ways that address a range of learning styles, presenting students with a number of ways to begin understanding the content.[8] Unfortunately, relatively few instruction librarians have training in pedagogy or learning style theory, and only 20 percent of respondents to one survey on library learning objects indicated that they attempted to incorporate multiple styles.[9]

Some scholars have criticized the idea of learning styles, questioning whether strong evidence exists that they have any real impact on student learning.[10] Many other educational theorists disagree, however, and in general, learning styles stand as a respected technique for understanding how student learning takes place.

Learning styles may have a significant impact on the quality of student learning. They can also have an effect on students' engagement and motivation, particularly when dealing with online learning material. A study by Speece found that "whatever the details of its conceptualization and measurement, learning style does have some impact on *attitudes* towards online classes [emphasis added]."[11] Since most of us serve as guest lecturers and library learning can often be seen as a (rarely graded) optional or supplemental class activity, this effect may have a greater significance to us than to a teacher who has grades and other motivational tools at her disposal.

Learning Styles: Three Models

Above I referred to learning styles as "a theory," but in fact there are many related theories and models that have emerged over the decades. Because educational scholars don't agree on a one hundred percent standardized definition of the term, there are varying approaches to modeling learning styles. There is no one correct or definitive model of learning styles; there are many ways to conceptualize or construct lenses through which to better understand students and learning.

A complete overview is beyond the scope of this book, but I've chosen three representative examples of models (plus some bonus examples specifically from the LIS field) that education scholars have used to illustrate learning styles. I chose these three because they occur frequently in the LIS literature, and while they have some conceptual overlap with each other, they illustrate some differences and contrasts between how scholars approach the idea of learning styles. Many other models would work just as well as examples, and the reference list for this chapter contains references that use other models.

Should you research and select a specific learning style model to design your guides around? Not necessarily. Some basic understanding of learning style theory—say, as much as you can get from this chapter—is useful, but it doesn't take extensive study and research to understand enough about the concept to improve your guides.

Teaching material doesn't have to be specifically designed around a single model in order to take advantage of the benefits of incorporating learning styles. Different learning style models do not work in opposition to each other: they can be combined and blended as the librarian thinks best for her audience and can work together to improve learning.[12]

Perceptual Preference Modality

The perceptual preference modality model is based on the idea that each student's inclination toward preferred sensory stimuli influences learning. It models student learning preferences according to sense-based groups:

- Auditory learners have a preference for verbal instruction and work well with guidance by sound, narration, or other audible direction. In a research guide context, this may mean they prefer tutorials or other audio-based materials.

- Visual learners prefer observational learning. In a situation involving online text, like the traditional library webpage, they tend to skim the page to seek out needed information. Illustrations and well-organized text with intentional cues may appeal to these learners (see chapter 4 on design and writing for some further ideas).
- Tactile learners and kinesthetic learners (which I group together here for simplicity) are attracted to interactivity. Both groups prefer to learn from experience; tactile learners tend to keep their hands moving (e.g., taking notes, doodling), and kinesthetic learners prefer whole-body movement. This seems like a difficult style to engage with web material, but these learners appreciate exploring a guide, clicking links and mousing over objects to discover information.[13]

Kolb Experiential Learning Model

Educational theorist David Kolb classifies learners according to his Experiential Learning Model along two axes (figure 3.1): active experimentation (testing new insights) versus reflective observation (considering new experience in the light of past experience), and abstract conceptualization (developing deep understanding based on experience) versus concrete experience (learning based on actual experiences).[14]

Learners who prefer concrete and active learning may be at a disadvantage in asynchronous online learning situations, so librarians should consider including elements that appeal to these learner types in particular: incorporating "concrete examples, demonstrations, theoretical elaborations and activities" can help keep more leaners engaged.[15]

Guides that take active/concrete learners into account could include elements like

- worked examples of live catalog/database searches to illustrate how searching works
- worksheets into which students can enter their own topics to brainstorm keywords
- quizzes or games using specific examples of research processes

This learning model also relates to the idea of chunking information from chapter 2 on learning objectives. Learners who favor reflective observation and abstract conceptualization may have an easier time taking material from short-term memory and processing it into long-term learning without experiencing cognitive overload and may cope better with larger and more complex information chunks.

Kolb Experiential Learning Model

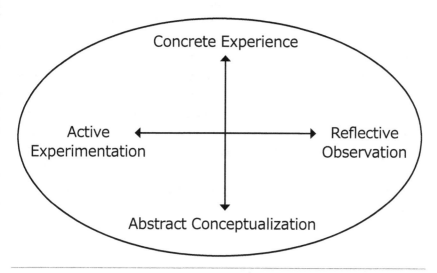

FIGURE 3.1

A simple visualization of the Kolb Experiential Learning model—learners are classified according to an active/reflective scale and an abstract/concrete one.

Gardner's Multiple Intelligences

Howard Gardner's model of learning styles is perhaps one of the best known. It emphasizes individual differences in modes of thinking, called multiple intelligences. According to this theory, each learner has different strengths classified along these criteria:

- *Logical-mathematical intelligence* is used to recognize patterns and in deductive reasoning and logical thinking.
- *Linguistic intelligence* governs expression and comprehension of verbal information.
- *Spatial intelligence* represents our ability to manipulate mental images in problem solving.
- *Musical intelligence* is used in recognizing and creating pitch and rhythm.

- *Bodily-kinesthetic intelligence* coordinates movement and physical activity.
- *Interpersonal and intrapersonal intelligence* is used in comprehension of feelings and intentions—one's own and others'.[16]

The most common approaches in educational design appeal exclusively to the first two intelligences, logical-mathematical and linguistic. It's difficult to see how some of these intelligences could be addressed in a research guide—musical intelligence stands out in particular—but others are not as obscure as they may seem. We've already seen that something as simple as exploring links and discovering information via mouseover increases the sense of interaction with a guide and appeal to physical learners like those with strong bodily-kinesthetic intelligence. The librarian may be able to appeal to interpersonal/intrapersonal-oriented learners by basing examples and explanations on real-world assignments, drawing connections between the more abstract ideas behind research and the actual needs and intentions of the student.

Applying Learning Style Theory to Library Research Guides

Matching research guide design to students' preferred styles of learning can make a difference. The nature and format in which information is presented to students has been shown to enhance student learning outcomes when matched to their learning style strengths.[17] In an ideal world, students might be able to choose among several formats to experience the material in the style of their choice.

Few librarians actually have training in best practices for designing online learning objects to address concerns such as learning styles.[18] Fortunately, in practical terms, instruction librarians need not become experts in learning style theory in order to create effective guides—a little knowledge goes a long way in this case.

Depending on the intended audience for a particular research guide and the librarian's knowledge of her students, it might be possible to tailor the guide to match the students' presumed learning styles to some extent. An extreme level of customization is difficult and unrealistic for the typical librarian to achieve—but also probably not necessary.

It would be impossible to cater to every student's specific preferred style, but library instructional resources "should reflect an understanding of individual differences by appropriately incorporating strategies for a variety of learning styles."[19] What matters most is keeping in mind that presenting information in ways that address a *variety* of styles can make your guides more effective at reaching a wider audience of students. In short, *framing your material in a variety of styles can help more students understand and use it.*

This can be as simple as providing your students with options such as images, video tutorials, interactive learning objects, and other alternatives to the intimidating, discouraging, and dull "wall of text" format that is unfortunately so prevalent in research guides. Even simple efforts like these can not only help learners who prefer differing styles process the information you're conveying on your guide, it can also draw attention to and reinforce key concepts, make guides more visually interesting and attractive, and encourage students to spend more time with the material in your guides.

This idea is particularly important in the online learning environment, where students cannot ask you for clarification or explanation. Students using research guides are not likely to be a "captive audience" as they are in a classroom instruction session, so they may see guides as supplemental or optional material and skip them if they find them confusing or problematic. Making guides engaging encourages students to actually use them. In fact, providing instructional materials that accommodate a range of learning styles is not only good pedagogical practice, it can help reduce students' library anxiety. Students with weaknesses in specific styles may be more susceptible to library anxiety, and addressing their style preferences can help the development of their information skills.[20]

Many researchers support the "matching hypothesis," which states that teachers should learn what their students' preferred styles are and adjust instruction to fit these styles as closely as possible in order to optimize lessons for students.[21] A difficulty for instruction librarians is the fact that we typically don't know students as well as their regular teacher does—often not at all, since we may meet students for only a single class. This makes it impossible for us to adjust guides to fit with students' learning styles. Fortunately, we need not tailor our guides to meet the needs of individual students in order to improve their effectiveness. Learning some basics of learning style theory allows us to create better guides not by adjusting guides to accommodate specific students, but by adjusting guides to be a better fit with a wider *range* of student profiles.

In fact, accommodating students' individual preferences is only one way to usefully apply learning styles, and maybe not even the most useful way. While learning styles may help librarians design guides to better appeal to a majority of students, they may also help us from other perspectives as well.

Accommodate the material, not the student. One or more styles may be well suited to a particular class or learning objective in a guide entirely independent of any student preferences. A guide on writing literature reviews may work well best in a textual format, but a guide teaching basic search processes might be better suited to include a flowchart or visual diagrams to help direct students through the choices and discrete stages of the process. A guide teaching a complicated software program might do well to include short tutorial videos to demonstrate how tasks look in action and provide audio narration to accompany the demo.[22]

Play to the teacher's strengths. Using learning style information doesn't improve a guide just by providing students with a more comfortable format. Being aware of our own preferred styles can also encourage us to work within those styles, hopefully creating better quality guides in the process. If you yourself are a strongly visual learner, take advantage of that preference and incorporate more diagrams and illustrations in your guide rather than limiting yourself to just bullet points and lists.

Recognize the teacher's shortfalls. Taking note of your own style preferences also helps you evaluate your guides to include enough diversity of format. If you have a preference for a kinesthetic style in your own learning, review your guide start to finish, making sure that a student who thinks sequentially won't be lost. Borrow ideas and (with permission) content from colleagues who use styles differently than you yourself do: many librarians would rather jump off a cliff than record their own voice in a video but have colleagues who are hams and love to narrate tutorials. If you're one of the former, see if your coworkers or counterparts at other institutions have produced multimedia that you can adopt or adapt for your own guides. Some of the design concepts in chapter 4 will also help you produce guides that don't drift too far in the direction of your preferred style to the extent of confusing or turning off users.

Play against students' strengths. While students may prefer information presented in particular styles, they face a constant challenge as learners to take on information in many different ways, not just in their style of choice. Providing students with some material in a variety of styles—even mismatched to their stronger styles—may actually help them strengthen their skills and develop new learning strategies by teaching them how to cope with lessons *not* specifically tailored to them. Some researchers argue that if students learn only in their preferred styles, it hinders their progress when they are forced to adapt to different styles.[23]

It seems clear that using learning styles in various aspects of library instruction can help to lessen library anxiety and improve student attitudes toward library instruction. Taking learning styles into account in some simple ways can help the library instructor reach students in ways that feel more comfortable and natural to them.

For many students, it may not make a significant difference what learning styles are used in designing a guide—or a class, for that matter— but others may have difficulty taking in large amounts of information via particular mediums, and for these students some attention to style can help improve their comprehension or at least their comfort level: "Most students learn with all their styles. However, some students may have unusual weaknesses in particular styles. It is these students who may have problems utilizing the library, and who may be more susceptible to high levels of library anxiety."[24]

Examples: Using Learning Styles in Research Guides

In practical terms, what should a library research guide include when taking account of learning styles? Let's look at specifics.

Simply put, the ideal guide should include a mix of elements and methods to more effectively reach the largest range of students. Many library guides focus too heavily on text and too much of it. Students in an online environment (as they all are when reading an online guide) need to be presented with information in a variety of formats, including text, aural, visual, and kinesthetic.[25]

Simple and useful guidelines for this approach can be found in the Universal Design for Learning (UDL) principles—a model of learning styles designed to reach a wide spectrum of students with diverse needs. UDL has been specifically adapted to the library instruction context by authors like Chodock and Dolinger and Zhong.[26] UDL recommends that library instructors do the following in their learning materials:

- "Provide multiple means of representation." Present content in a variety of modes: not just textual, but visual, graphic, or auditory.
- "Provide multiple means of action and expression." Give students multiple opportunities to express or demonstrate the material they learn.
- "Provide multiple means of engagement." Offer a variety of ways to actively involve students in learning.[27]

Let's examine some ideas for how a librarian might approach applying these guidelines to some individual styles. Again, the following is by no means an exhaustive list of styles, just some common examples. I've chosen a small variety based on studies in the LIS literature and their applicability to the research guide format and have intentionally chosen some styles that can be seen as contrasts to one another.

How to Evaluate Research

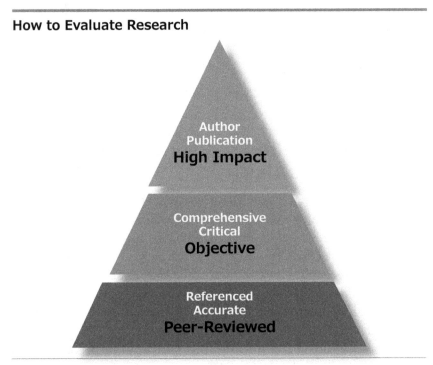

FIGURE 3.2

This image provides an easy visual reference for concepts explained in more detail on the guide. (Queensland University of Technology, http://airs.library.qut.edu.au/3/2/) (cc) BY

Visual

This style may be the easiest to address in the online environment (figure 3.2). The web is a heavily visual medium, after all. It's relatively simple to incorporate images into a webpage. In fact, to generalize a bit, most students rely heavily on visual cues like graphics and images to interpret webpages and look for the information they need.[28]

Images, the most common form of visual cue in research guides, can be used in different ways to enhance a web guide: as visual emphasis, to draw attention to specific information, and to reinforce or reframe ideas presented in the text. Later we'll look at some specific ideas for using visual design in guides to emphasize important information, but in short, any sort of graphic can break up large chunks of text and "pull" the reader's eye to a spot on the page.

But images can be used as more than visual indicators to get the reader's attention: they can actually work as teaching tools. Many library guides direct the reader through a process or series of steps or stages, and creating a visual representation of those steps can help clarify a process. A flowchart is a clear example (figure 3.3)—each stage in a research process can be represented discretely, with a path in the form of lines or arrows indicating how the student should proceed from one step to the next.

Images can also be used to illustrate new concepts for students: Venn diagrams can describe nonverbally how the contents of different databases relate to each other or how broader, narrower, and related subject headings compare and overlap.

Annotated screenshots can be tremendously helpful to visual learners. A textual description of a search screen might describe what students should pay attention to while doing research, but an actual image of the real screen—with labels and callout—can give students absolute reassurance that the example matches their own procedure or indicate features and tools that they shouldn't overlook. Comparing a screenshot with the live database helps students verify the accuracy of their steps against the librarian's instructions.[29]

It may be difficult for some students—those whose first language is not English, for example, or students using the library for the first time, or those who strongly lean toward visual learning—to closely follow textual instructions. Images transcend language and can help overcome misunderstandings based on vocabulary or phrasing.

Research Flow Chart

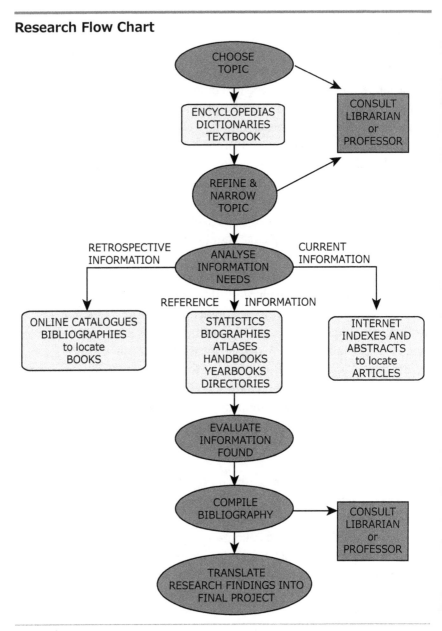

FIGURE 3.3

A flowchart provides a visual representation of a process as well as an easy-to-follow sequential summary. (Judy Vogt, University of Lethbridge Library, http://uleth.ca/lib/classes/ed4950/step1.html)

On the other hand, visual learners are less likely to explore the guide's content with the mouse, preferring to read (or skim) the page fully before deciding where to click. Strongly visual learners may miss information contained in a mouseover or tooltip or worked examples such as canned searches that require clicking a link to activate.[30]

Interactive/Kinesthetic/Tactile

Interactive, kinesthetic, and tactile learner types (figure 3.4) come from different style models, but I group them together here since to generalize a bit, they share some common traits. These styles of learners tend to learn from real-life experience or something like it: "learn by doing" is the phrase to keep in mind. These and related learning styles are slightly more challenging to accommodate in a web guide, but with a little thought and creativity, they don't have to be difficult to address.

Search Strategy Builder

The Search Strategy Builder is a tool designed to teach you how to create a search string using Boolean logic. While it is not a database and is not designed to input a search, you should be able to cut and paste the results into most databases' search boxes.

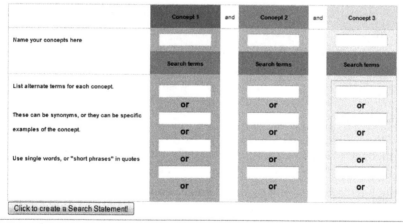

FIGURE 3.4

This search builder tool by University of Arizona Libraries would appeal to interactive learners. Students can experiment with entering synonyms and related search terms and see how they join up to form Boolean statements of varying complexity. (http://library.arizona.edu/help/tutorials/searchBuilder.html)

These students tend to prefer activities. In contrast to visual learners, they are likely to explore guides by following links, browsing through pages, and clicking anything that looks interactive. Hand motion and screen movement stimulates their attention, and they are more likely to discover information provided in tooltips and mouseovers.[31]

To help these learners, provide them with things like

- tasks and exercises to work through
- working search boxes
- steps to follow
- reactive elements to click
- links to other useful pages and resources

Embedded games and interactive quizzes would fit well with these learning styles. Structuring a guide to allow for independent navigation—clear sections for students to explore and refer to at their own pace and in their own sequence—also works well. This is problematic for long video tutorials without chapter markers; breaking up longer tutorials into shorter videos that can be selected individually helps solve this problem.

Interactivity of some sort (figure 3.5) is actually a very common learning preference: one library study showed that a majority of students desired multiple paths to find needed information and interactive opportunities in online learning objects, but only a tiny percentage of libraries provided them. In fact, the students who had the most success performing a search task were those who had previously tried an interactive online exercise.[32]

Auditory

Auditory is another example of a learning style that doesn't come to mind immediately when we think about learning material situated on the web. Auditory learners prefer sound-based or verbal instruction as guidance, though the typical webpage includes only visual or textual information.

It's relatively easy to incorporate audio narration into any video tutorial. In fact, this has the added advantage of giving students two "streams" of information to process in parallel, to reinforce the material in a way that works well for most learners: visual demonstration or textual instructions on the screen, with a librarian giving verbal explanation as the tutorial proceeds. A pure audio file might be less useful to most learners than one that also includes video, but on the other hand it would be useful for students who prefer to download learning materials—like a recorded class lecture—to listen on mobile devices.

Auditory learning options need not be high-tech at all: don't forget to include a phone number for the instruction librarian or the reference desk so students can get verbal instructions.[33]

Interactive Article

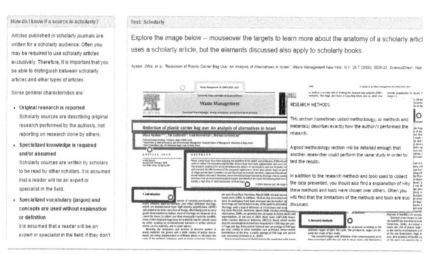

FIGURE 3.5

This page contains textual information on the left reinforced by visual/interactive elements on the right. As students explore sections of the article (highlighted by colored boxes in the original), definitions and explanations appear. (Meagan Kinsley, American University Library, http://subjectguides.library.american.edu/c.php?g=175252&p=1155680)

Sequential

Sequential learners prefer to have information presented to them in logical, linear steps. They appreciate the sense that the librarian is guiding them through a process from start to finish.[34]

On the surface, this sounds like a contradiction to the advice given for interactive learners, who prefer to choose their own path, but in fact the two styles can easily be accommodated in the same guide. Clear labeled sections of a guide work well for both styles, allowing the student to either progress from beginning to end or choose individual sections by referring forward and backward as needed.

Sequential Guide

Junior English Research Project: Day One

Day One	Day Two	Day Three	Day Four	Day Five	Day Six	Day Seven

Topic Reflection Handout	Current Controversies Databases Checklist
• 📄 Topic Reflection and Research Instructions	• 📄 Checklist for Current Controversies Databases **Type of Source:** periodical articles, overviews, and statistics

FIGURE 3.6

This high school English guide is laid out to appeal strongly to sequential learners, suggesting a literal day-by-day research plan for students to follow. (Glenbrook North High School Library, http://gbn.glenbrook. libguides.com/juniorenglish)

Guides designed with some of chapter 2's ideas about learning objectives, scaffolding, and chunking in mind should be comfortable for sequential learners. These are natural and logical ways to provide students with a guided progression through the research project. Provide students with a linear model to help them understand the steps and stages involved, even if the real-life process tends to be messier and less neatly sequential! A neat progression of steps helps their comprehension of what objectives they need to accomplish.

Drawbacks and Practical Concerns

Designing guides for learning styles is a new approach for many librarians, and there are practical concerns to be considered before rethinking guide creation. For most of us, there is a learning curve involved as we get up to speed on even the basics of learning style theory and the associated ideas from educational research. Unless you're brand-new to instruction work, you likely already have many research guides set up and running that you're hesitant to scrap completely and start over from scratch.

Does designing guides based on learning styles take more work? Not necessarily, over the long term. The greatest effort involved in addressing learning styles comes early on in the process: assessing, at least informally, the needs of students and how you already cater to them in your guides and considering what styles you might have left out based on your old approach. Once you've begun to work the idea of learning styles into your guides, continuing to keep them in mind begins to come naturally and easily.

Also keep in mind that this isn't an all-or-nothing proposition. Revising and updating guides based on a new approach doesn't have to happen all at once, and probably can't. Rethinking old guides can happen bit by bit: adding a new tutorial video, replacing a large chunk of text with an explanatory graphic, supplementing long instructions with active links and worked examples are all improvements that can easily happen over time and don't require scrapping large amounts of existing work. For most instruction librarians, demand for new classes and content comes in steadily over time, and these new classes can serve as opportunities to approach guides from a new perspective.

Many ideas for addressing learning styles involve creating non-text media such as images, audio, and video. It's often true that the more media-based the content, the more work it is to update: it's usually more effort to produce a video than it is to write a few paragraphs of text. However, producing media isn't simply a one-to-one equivalent tradeoff for text content. Media content may be a more efficient way to convey information to many learners. It may attract more users to your guides, and as we'll discuss in chapter 4, it may be a better way to draw users' attention to the most important sections of your guide pages. It can also help condense more information into a smaller space on the screen and may ensure that important content isn't pushed down the page where students are less likely to read it.

Investing some extra time and effort up front can also pay off in the long term. In most cases, new content (visual, textual, or other) that you create for one guide can be reused for multiple guides. A graphic on reading call numbers can probably be used to replace text that appears in other guides, and a tutorial on locating articles will have applications many places in your instructional content. If you're directly addressing students' learning outcomes, as we discussed in chapter 2, then a good deal of your guide content will be specific to a particular and can't be reused verbatim, but you will likely find that a large amount of it can be repurposed with only minor changes and customization.

Summing Up: Some Simple Best Practices

Keep all this in mind when you're creating new guides, and you'll find that using learning styles in your guides isn't nearly as difficult or time-consuming as it may seem at first. Consider some fundamental principles as you design your guides, try out some new techniques, and be prepared to adjust or disregard any of this information based on your first-hand knowledge of and experience with your students.

You can't adapt every guide perfectly to each individual student's learning style preferences. That's okay. Rather, the intent should be to appeal to a wide range of learner types.

In order for a guide to address a variety of learning styles, it should ideally include a mix of text, audiovisual media and interactive elements without relying too heavily on any one medium. A few points to remember:

- Visual information may mean moving video or still images. Ideally, auditory and visual information should include text captioning, both to reinforce the lesson and to improve accessibility.
- Clear navigation arranged in a logical fashion provides a sequential path through any processes or steps. The user should have access to any arbitrary point in the sequence they wish, based on their needs at any given moment. Their research process may not mirror your neat sequence.
- Interactivity comes in forms like worked examples, exercises, quizzes, functional search boxes, or other means for the user to use the guide in ways other than just reading it. Interactivity can be as simple as clickable links—this helps make the guide a useful resource that students are more likely to return to.

For many of our students, learning to do research is an entirely new experience. We can help them through this experience in a comfortable, comprehensible, and useful way by strengthening and adapting our guides to meet them halfway. "Our job is to make the Web site and the resources accessible for as many of them as we can, and we can do this better by understanding how people learn."[35]

Notes

1. Lori S. Mestre, *Designing Effective Library Tutorials* (Oxford: Chandos, 2012), 3.
2. Lori S. Mestre, "Student Preference for Tutorial Design," *Reference Services Review* 40, no. 2 (May 2012): 260, doi:10.1108/00907321211228318.
3. Seval Fer, "Demographic Characteristics and Intellectual Styles," in *Handbook of Intellectual Styles*, ed. Li-fang Zhang, Robert J. Sternberg, and Stephen Rayner (New York: Springer, 2012), 110.
4. Lori S. Mestre, "Matching Up Learning Styles with Learning Objects," *Journal of Library Administration* 50, no. 7/8 (December 2010): 812, doi:10.1080/01930826.2010.488975; Mark Speece, "Learning Style, Culture and Delivery Mode in Online Distance Education," *US–China Education Review A* 2, no. 1 (January 2012): 6–7.
5. Mestre, *Designing Effective Library Tutorials*, 4.
6. Ibid., 8.
7. Ibid.
8. Ibid., 12.
9. Mestre, "Matching Up Learning Styles with Learning Objects," 810, 817.
10. Carol Evans and Michael Waring, "Applications of Styles in Educational Instruction and Assessment," in *Handbook of Intellectual Styles*, ed. Li-fang Zhang, Robert J. Sternberg, and Stephen Rayner (New York: Springer, 2012), 310.
11. Speece, "Learning Style, Culture and Delivery Mode," 5.
12. May Ying Chau, "Connecting Learning Styles and Multiple Intelligences Theories through Learning Strategies," *Libres: Library & Information Science Research Electronic Journal* 16, no. 1 (March 2006), http://libres-ejournal.info/843.
13. Terri A. Holtze, "Applying Learning Style Theory to Web Page Design," *Internet Reference Services Quarterly* 5, no. 2 (April 2000): 74.
14. Experience Based Learning Systems homepage, 2014, http://learningfromexperience.com; Mestre, "Matching Up Learning Styles with Learning Objects," 811–12.
15. Yunfei Du, "Exploring the Difference between 'Concrete' and 'Abstract,'" *Journal of Library & Information Services in Distance Learning* 1, no. 3 (September 2004): 53, 61, doi:10.1300/J192v01n03_04.
16. Mestre, *Designing Effective Library Tutorials*, 24–25.
17. Evans and Waring, "Applications of Styles in Educational Instruction and Assessment," 312.

18. Mestre, "Matching Up Learning Styles with Learning Objects," 810–11; Li-fang Zhang, Robert J. Sternberg, and Stephen Rayner, eds., *Handbook of Intellectual Styles* (New York: Springer, 2012).
19. Anthony J. Onwuegbuzie and Qun G. Jiao, "The Relationship between Library Anxiety and Learning Styles among Graduate Students," *Library & Information Science Research* 20, no. 3 (September 1998): 246.
20. Ibid., 237.
21. Mestre, *Designing Effective Library Tutorials*, 8–9.
22. Ibid., 10.
23. Ibid.
24. Onwuegbuzie and Jiao, "The Relationship between Library Anxiety and Learning Styles," 237.
25. Mestre, "Matching Up Learning Styles with Learning Objects," 808.
26. Ted Chodock and Elizabeth Dolinger, "Applying Universal Design to Information Literacy," *Reference & User Services Quarterly* 49, no. 1 (Fall 2009): 24–32; Ying Zhong, "Universal Design for Learning (UDL) in Library Instruction," *College & Undergraduate Libraries* 19, no. 1 (2012): 33–45, doi:1 0.1080/10691316.2012.652549.
27. "UDL Guidelines—Version 2.0," National Center on Universal Design for Learning, 2013, http://www.udlcenter.org/aboutudl/udlguidelines.
28. Mestre, *Designing Effective Library Tutorials*, 78–79.
29. Ibid.
30. Holtze, "Applying Learning Style Theory to Web Page Design," 75.
31. Ibid.
32. Mestre, "Matching Up Learning Styles with Learning Objects," 824–25.
33. Holtze, "Applying Learning Style Theory to Web Page Design," 74–75.
34. Mestre, *Designing Effective Library Tutorials*, 26.
35. Holtze, "Applying Learning Style Theory to Web Page Design," 73.

References

Chau, May Ying. "Connecting Learning Styles and Multiple Intelligences Theories through Learning Strategies: An On Line Tutorial for Library Instruction." *Libres: Library & Information Science Research Electronic Journal* 16, no. 1 (March 2006). http://libres-ejournal.info/843. .

Chodock, Ted, and Elizabeth Dolinger. "Applying Universal Design to Information Literacy: Teaching Students Who Learn Differently at Landmark College." *Reference & User Services Quarterly* 49, no. 1 (Fall 2009): 24–32.

Du, Yunfei. "Exploring the Difference between 'Concrete' and 'Abstract': Learning Styles in LIS Distance Education." *Journal of Library & Infor-*

mation Services in Distance Learning 1, no. 3 (September 2004): 51–64. doi:10.1300/J192v01n03_04.

Evans, Carol, and Michael Waring. "Applications of Styles in Educational Instruction and Assessment." In *Handbook of Intellectual Styles: Preferences in Cognition, Learning, and Thinking*, edited by Li-fang Zhang, Robert J. Sternberg, and Stephen Rayner, 295–327. New York: Springer, 2012.

Experience Based Learning Systems. Homepage, 2014. http://learningfromexperience.com.

Fer, Seval. "Demographic Characteristics and Intellectual Styles." In *Handbook of Intellectual Styles: Preferences in Cognition, Learning, and Thinking*, edited by Li-fang Zhang, Robert J. Sternberg, and Stephen Rayner, 109–30. New York: Springer, 2012.

Holtze, Terri A. "Applying Learning Style Theory to Web Page Design." *Internet Reference Services Quarterly* 5, no. 2 (April 2000): 71–80.

Mestre, Lori S. *Designing Effective Library Tutorials: A Guide for Accommodating Multiple Learning Styles*. Oxford: Chandos, 2012.

———. "Matching Up Learning Styles with Learning Objects: What's Effective?" *Journal of Library Administration* 50, no. 7/8 (December 2010): 808–29. doi:10.1080/01930826.2010.488975.

———. "Student Preference for Tutorial Design: A Usability Study." *Reference Services Review* 40, no. 2 (May 2012): 258–76. doi:10.1108/00907321211228318.

National Center on Universal Design for Learning. "UDL Guidelines—Version 2.0," 2013. http://www.udlcenter.org/aboutudl/udlguidelines.

Onwuegbuzie, Anthony J., and Qun G. Jiao. "The Relationship between Library Anxiety and Learning Styles among Graduate Students: Implications for Library Instruction." *Library & Information Science Research* 20, no. 3 (September 1998): 235–49.

Speece, Mark. "Learning Style, Culture and Delivery Mode in Online Distance Education." *US–China Education Review A* 2, no. 1 (January 2012): 1–12.

Zhang, Li-fang, Robert J. Sternberg, and Stephen Rayner, eds. *Handbook of Intellectual Styles: Preferences in Cognition, Learning, and Thinking*. New York: Springer, 2012.

Zhong, Ying. "Universal Design for Learning (UDL) in Library Instruction." *College & Undergraduate Libraries* 19, no. 1 (2012): 33–45. doi:10.1080/10691316.2012.652549.

CHAPTER 4

Designing and Writing for Better Usability

Introduction

UNLESS THE INSTRUCTION LIBRARIAN is also the library's web administrator, it's very likely that she wasn't trained as a web designer. Librarians are not expert in visual design, and we're not trained in how to write for the web—a very different kind of writing from the academic papers we had to produce in grad school and for our own research—and both of these elements play an important part in how our users see our research guides, whether they feel comfortable using them, and whether they find them useful or just confusing.

Observation, teaching, and looking at many research guides leads me to believe that librarians tend toward a couple of characteristics that *don't* make us good web designers.

First of all, we're highly text-oriented. Librarians are comfortable with reading and writing to an extent that novice students may not be. It often doesn't occur to us that a detailed paragraph of instructions might look like a long and intimidating block of difficult material to a user who's less comfortable with reading, less experienced with research, and less familiar with our terminology.

Secondly, we're completionists. We're accustomed to consulting lengthy reference works and bibliographies so that we can zero in on a single needed piece of information. We often implicitly believe that it's better to include too much information than too little, that a long list is better because it's more comprehensive and more likely to include the needed resource. We think (perhaps unconsciously) of a research guide as a complete collection of all the information a user might potentially need on a topic. For a novice user, the guides we produce may create paralysis and confusion because novices don't know where to start, or don't know how to select one resource over another.

Bearing in mind that these are generalizations, think about how these characteristics of the "librarian brain" could affect how we put together webpages like research guides.

Research guides (and webpages in general) are rarely laid out as simply as a printed page of text. The reader doesn't always have a clear starting point; the eye can't count on going straight to the top left corner and working right and downward. There are usually multiple columns and multiple potential starting points on the page (figure 4.1). There are probably many headings, links, and points of departure visible on a single screen.

A Page of Text with a Single Column

tuned and broken at the capstan bars. Then he rapped on the door with a bit of stick like a handspike that he carried, and when my father appeared, called roughly for a glass of rum. This, when it was brought to him, he drank slowly, like a connoisseur, lingering on the taste and still looking about him at the cliffs and up at our signboard.

"This is a handy cove," says he at length; "and a pleasant sittyated grog-shop. Much company, mate?"

My father told him no, very little company, the more was the pity.

"Well, then," said he, "this is the berth for me. Here you, matey," he cried to the man who trundled the barrow; "bring up alongside and help up my chest. I'll stay here a bit," he continued. "I'm a plain man; rum and bacon and eggs is what I want, and that head up there for to watch ships off. What you mought call me? You mought call me captain. Oh, I see what you're at--there"; and he threw down three or four gold pieces on the threshold. "You can tell me when I've worked through that," says he, looking as fierce as a commander.

And indeed bad as his clothes were and coarsely as he spoke, he had none of the appearance of a man who sailed before the mast, but seemed like a mate or skipper accustomed to be obeyed or to strike. The man who came with the barrow told us the mail had set him down the

More Complex Layout of a Research Guide

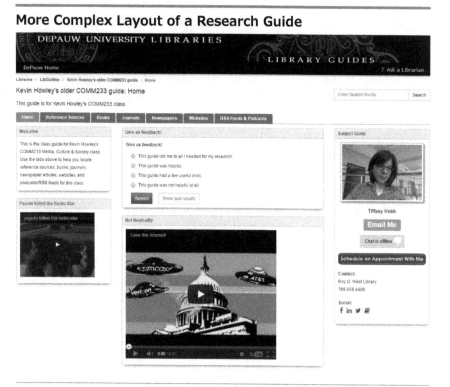

FIGURE 4.1

The printed page of a book gives the reader a clear start-to-finish path through the information (left). A typical research guide has many potential starting points and paths through the information and needs some visual indicators to indicate where the reader should look (above). (Tiffany Hebb, DePauw University, http://libguides.depauw.edu/comm233-howley)

Content management software like LibGuides or WordPress can help us with some of the very basics of design: our web administrator usually sets up the colors, fonts, and other fundamental elements of design. Usually our research guides CMS is set up to match the rest of the library website in some fundamental ways: colors, banner, perhaps navigation menus, and that sort of thing. This is important for a number of reasons: it visually indicates to our users that they haven't left the library's site (even if the guides are hosted on a different web server from the main site, as is often the case), it provides a consistent experience that doesn't distract students from the content, and so on.

As guide authors, however, we usually still have enough control over the appearance of the guide to make a mess of things if we don't think about what we're doing. Basic elements of the user's experience are entirely in the hands of the librarian creating the guide, and that's what we'll examine in this chapter—things like good use of images, providing visual cues to starting points, creating text that is easy to read on the web, and keeping your guide's design clear, consistent, and concise.

None of this requires any technical knowledge, and all of it can make a big difference to the user.

I'll start with a quick overview of user experience (UX), an important principle for anyone creating web content to understand. We'll then examine simple principles of visual design, clarity and conciseness, how web users read, and how librarians can use that information to craft better text for research guides.

While this chapter is based more heavily on web design principles than on educational theory, don't forget to bear in mind our previous discussions about learning styles, chunking, and information overload—you'll find that these ideas from two different fields all go nicely hand-in-hand.

User Experience

What Is UX?

An important idea in creating webpages is user experience, often abbreviated UX. UX design for the web is about making a site—whether a library's main website, a catalog or search tool, or in our case, a research guide—as easy, comfortable, and natural to use as possible.

Good UX means that the site's design "gets out of the way" of the information on the page. The user shouldn't have to think about how the site works; it should be as clear and intuitive as possible where to find the needed information. The design of the page is "transparent," not placing a barrier between the student and the information. Achieving good UX means that distractions from this goal should be minimized.

If students don't have an immediate positive user experience on our guides, it's a cold and cruel fact that they simply won't use them and will go elsewhere on the web after a few seconds.

Schmidt and Etches's book *User Experience (UX) Design for Libraries* is an excellent examination of how to apply these ideas to library web pages, including several principles that are particularly applicable to research guide creators:

- *Less is less (and that's a good thing).* Make the guide as small as possible—visually, textually, and in its topic focus—to make it easier to find information.
- *Patrons don't read library websites, they scan them.* Present your information in easy-to-skim chunks, using elements like emphasized key terms and bulleted lists, to enable your students to find needed information quickly. They will not read your guide start to finish.
- *Library websites are for library users, not librarians.* Keep this one in mind at all times! Look at your guide from the user's point of view.
- *When in doubt, leave it out.* "You should be able to strongly articulate reasons for including every single thing that's on your library's site." Delete anything that's on your guide only because it might come in handy, not because you're sure it's relevant.[1]

Most other guidelines for good UX in library sites give compatible advice. Hemmig recommends principles of research guide design that include

- "Short pages that do not require scrolling;
- Consistency of page design within the guide;…
- Avoidance of long, alphabetical or unsorted lists;
- Clear indication of the destinations of links;…
- Simplicity in structure and language;
- An obvious, familiar main page; …
- Appropriate, logical access points;"[2]

… all of which fit into these fundamental design ideas: brevity, clarity, simplicity, and usability.

UX and Online Instruction

Content is not all that matters when information is delivered to a guide user. Guide authors have to give care not just in crafting *what* information is given. Composition (how the information is arranged and presented) also plays a key role.

All classroom teachers know that presentation makes a difference in how students learn in the classroom. If the instructor speaks in a monotone, lectures nonstop without engaging the class with questions and discussion, or is difficult to understand, students will tune him out even if the class material itself is otherwise flawless.

When thinking of research guides in the context of their use as a teaching tool, good user experience is more than just a nice-looking webpage. It's the equivalent of good classroom presentation. It doesn't make up for a bad teacher, but it can make sure that a good teacher does a better job at keeping students engaged and helps the material get through in a useful way.

In a visual/textual medium like a webpage, good presentation includes elements of design like visual composition, use of images and color, and even careful editing of text to take into account the fact that students read the web differently from the printed page.

A few ideas to keep in mind about user experience from a teaching perspective:

Research guides serve a particular instructional function—often an introductory or basic-level one. With some exceptions, the guide user is most often a novice researcher. They don't have to be comprehensive and all-inclusive; at their best, they serve as a jumping-off point for the researcher. "Pathfinders are not exhaustive guides to the literature. Pathfinders are designed for beginners who need help finding the fundamental literature of a subject."[3] Conciseness and simplicity are virtues.

The look at learning objectives in chapter 2 can give you some guidance in achieving this focus. Guidelines for web writers suggest cutting the first draft of text by as much as 75 percent, which seems like a huge amount to condense. Using the UX principle of "When in doubt, leave it out" in conjunction with relevant and unambiguous learning objectives helps tremendously. "Setting instructional goals as a starting point will help to streamline and focus the content of the learning object and decide what is essential to include and what is not."[4]

Not only does defining an instructional goal for your guide help you make editorial decisions about what to include and omit, a more specific focus helps the user achieve more clarity. "Defining the scope of a pathfinder and keeping it manageable helps users to know whether it is appropriate for their needs and allows the pathfinder to be reasonably comprehensive without being excessively complex."[5] Clarity also helps bring confidence to users who may be suffering from library anxiety. Well-designed UX allows students to choose what parts of the guide to use, and in what order. "The hypertext medium was created in order to empower the reader to be able to select his or her own pathway through information. Traditional library instruction in a class context usually follows the instructor's pre-planned organization."[6]

Good UX that doesn't provide barriers to usability helps give the student a self-guided learning experience to complement the classroom experience. Too often, library pages force the student to adapt to unfamiliar material ("despite real concern for the user's needs it remains the user who is reoriented to conform to the needs of the system"[7]), and offering this sort of self-directed material helps counter that forced adaptation and put some control of the learning process into the student's hands.

Visual Design for Nondesigners

The visual design of a research guide—images, the use of space, layout—affects more than just the guide's surface prettiness. Visual design has a real and significant impact on user experience and learning effectiveness.

The word *attractive* comes up in lots of discussions about visual design. This sounds like a superficial term to use in the context of instructional design, but consider: to make our guides more effective and useful, they need to be attractive and appealing, not cluttered or confusing. "Attractive systems are those that work better—as librarians we're assisting people in stressful situations, learning new things, and facing deadlines,"[8] situations in which the page's design needs to "get out of the way" and foreground the instructional material itself. When it comes to web design and user experience, attractive, clear, and useful design goes hand-in-hand with useful content.

User studies back up this assertion. A group of University of British Columbia librarians had students use a range of research guides from different libraries, created using different CMS software, and asked them to rank their favorite guides and prioritize important guide characteristics (figure 4.2):

> [Students] generally chose the one they had ranked as highest in visual appearance. This relationship showed that while content and comprehension are important, visual appeal can be a deciding factor in determining which guides students would most likely use....

[One student commented that] "The format is very clear and neat. The first two webpages just make me feel dizzy. Too many words on it—very messy." The overwhelmingly positive response for this characteristic showed that basic principles of good web design must be followed.[9]

Hintz Survey Results

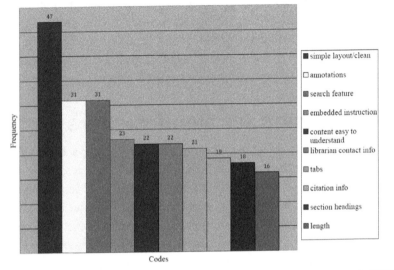

FIGURE 4.2

This survey by Hintz et al. indicated that students strongly preferred guides with a simple and clean layout—a preference that overshadowed all other characteristics.

Using Images

Using images well is an important element of designing a good research guide. Looking back at chapter 3, it's clear that including images is a simple way to make a guide appealing to a wider variety of learning styles. Even those learners who prefer styles that might seem opposed to visual learning, like those with a preference for written information, usually look at the visuals on a guide first and then go to the text if the images don't contain what they need.[10]

Images serve a number of different functions—not at all mutually exclusive—in a guide.

Simplest and perhaps most commonly, an image can serve as a visual "signpost," an indicator to students that they are in the right place for the information they seek. This is easy to do (figure 4.3). It can be as simple as locating a photo or illustration relevant to the subject of the guide: a portrait of Lincoln for a US history guide, a photo of Michelangelo's *David* for a Renaissance art guide, or an illustration of a DNA double helix for a microbiology guide.

Shakespeare Guide

FIGURE 4.3

The images on the home page of this Shakespeare guide immediately tell the student that they're in the right place. (Georgia Highlands College, http://getlibraryhelp.highlands.edu/Shakespeare)

An image that serves solely as a design element, like a photograph or symbol that doesn't add any new substantive information to the guide, will draw the attention and then "release" it, attracting the reader to the surrounding text. This type of image can still be useful to include! For example, an illustration of a molecule might not give students any new library information, but could instantly assure a student at a glance—without having to visually scan an information-dense page—that he has found a guide relevant to his biochemistry course. A series of guides for different courses could be laid out similarly to one another but with different illustrations to give users an instant means of differentiating them and indicating the topic of the guide.

Place an image like this near the top of the guide where it's visible in its entirety on a typical browser screen without having to page down (see "Above the Fold" below), and that's all there is to it. It's the same principle that makes icons on a computer screen or symbols on a road sign efficient ways to convey information: we can often spot and interpret the meaning of a picture more quickly than we can pick out relevant text, especially on a screen that's *full* of text.

Images can also be a more substantive means of conveying information—in a chart or diagram, or in a how-to illustration (figure 4.4). Diagrams and charts, when done well, can illustrate concepts visually that would be more difficult to explain in pure text. Guides including explanations of Boolean search logic often include Venn diagrams, for example, but there are other library-relevant topics that can benefit from a visual illustration of their concepts. The illustration of the literature search process in Figure 4.5 quickly conveys to the guide user the idea that research informs the choice and evolution of topics, which in turn informs the next phase of searching. Explaining the concept textually for students would probably take a paragraph or more, and might not be as clear. Including both text and an illustration helps reinforce the ideas, with each version of the information supporting the message of the other.

This type of image serves still serves as a design element, affecting the overall look of the page, but also as an instructional element. An image that's also an illustrative figure—a how-to diagram or a screenshot—is likely to retain the eye longer since it contains more information than one that's purely there to attract the reader's gaze. On the other hand, the more informational images on a page, the more cognitive load you're adding to what the reader takes in, so keep a balance in mind and don't overwhelm the student.

Zotero-JSTOR

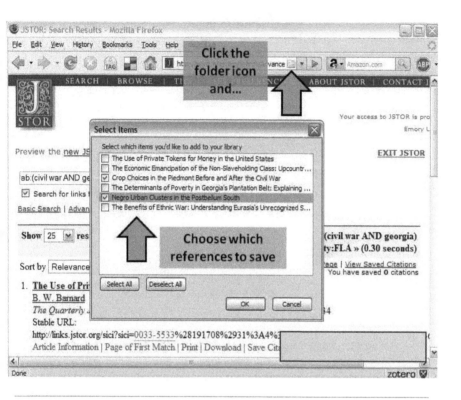

FIGURE 4.4

This illustration indicates the steps of a process that might be less clear if described in text and gives the user a concrete example to compare with what they see on their own screen. (Jason Puckett, http://research.library.gsu.edu/zotero)

Students in one library's user study (figure 4.6) "commented that they want to be able to skim and quickly find what they need. Therefore they suggested that the images be clear, crisp, large, and zoomed to the critical features. They would prefer that the steps be numbered inside the image…. Images should also match what they will see when they get to the real product."[11]

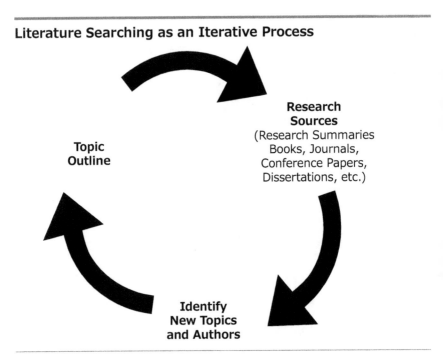

Literature Searching as an Iterative Process

FIGURE 4.5

This image concisely illustrates a concept about literature searches in order to supplement accompanying text. (University of Colorado, http://publishnotperish.org/module3/literature_search.htm)

Focal Points

Even though we try as hard as possible to make guides concise, easy to read, and clear, we frequently present a lot of information on a single page and there may sometimes be no way to avoid that. Students often have difficulty knowing where to start when presented with a guide page. Visual elements can be used to nonverbally direct the eye to chosen areas on a page so that the reader naturally finds key information and starting points.

Not only is it important to understand how to direct the reader toward important spots on the page, you should also be aware of elements on your page (possibly beyond your control) that might be drawing the reader's attention away from where you want it to go.

How can a guide author best direct users so they can find what they need quickly and efficiently? An easy way is by using *focal points*: areas of a page to which the eye is naturally drawn and from which the reader proceeds naturally through the guide.

Essential Parts of a Process

Start making sense of your network

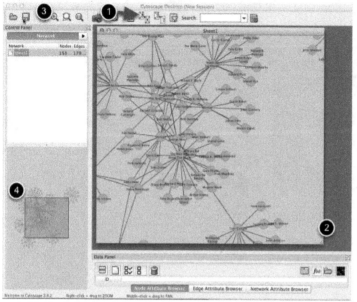

1. As a start, click on the little network diagram (hover over for a tool tip) to create a force-directed layout. Already that's much better!
2. Expand the size of your sheet by clicking and dragging the corner.
3. Zoom in by clicking on the magnifying glass and then clicking on the diagram.
4. Magnify different parts of your network by dragging around the shaded window

FIGURE 4.6

This image shows all the essential parts of a process, with numbered steps to indicate exactly what to do where. (Miriam Posner of UCLA, http://miriamposner.com/blog/visualize-a-network-of-film-casts-and-crews)

For our purposes, a focal point is any area on the screen that contrasts with its surroundings in terms of brightness, color, or design. High visual contrast pulls the gaze to that spot on the screen and unconsciously indicates to the reader that this is an important place and a potential starting point (or next point of interest).

Images are an easy element to use as focal points (figure 4.7). Typical guide content will be black text on a white background, so nearly any image placed on a page serves as a contrasting feature that will naturally pull the attention that way.

Focal Points

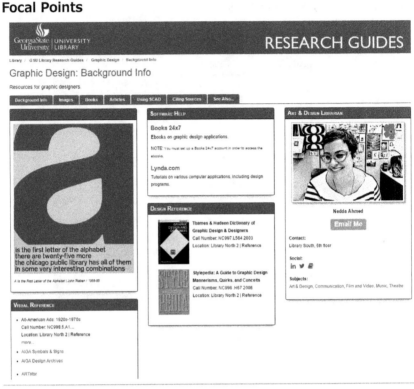

FIGURE 4.7

Each image on this guide is a focal point that draws attention to that area of the guide, starting with the large A, both because it's the largest and because it is at top left, a natural starting point. Attention naturally proceeds to the smaller images from there. This is a useful way to direct the reader to important places on the page. (Nedda Ahmed of Georgia State University, http://research.library.gsu.edu/graphicdesign)

This doesn't mean only images, though. *Any visual component* of a page that contrasts with its surrounding field can serve as a focal area, including an empty space. A block of text surrounded by more white space than usual will also draw the eye, subtly emphasizing its importance. (In fact, contrasting text in formats like **bold** or *italics* serves as a small and subtle focal area within a paragraph, which is why we use this method to emphasize important words and phrases.) If you have embedded videos on your page, remember that until you press Play, to the eye the still video is just another image—and another visual focus.

Most pages have multiple focal points. Most readers will start skimming near the top left of the page, so even without any visual cues this is a natural focus area. A high-contrast visual element in the top left reinforces this tendency—but that can be balanced or opposed with another focal area in the lower right to make sure that students don't miss an important section.

Many less obvious focal points appear on every page: headers in a larger font, blocks of color, menus, and other design elements. Just remain aware of which ones have the strongest influence over where the reader looks: the largest, boldest, and highest contrast areas. Tone down these spots (by removing images or simplifying your use of color, for example) if the page becomes too busy and confusing, and consider adding one or two if there's nothing to visually differentiate one area of the page from another.

Tip: Mark Up Your Screenshots with PowerPoint

You don't need Photoshop or other specialized software to annotate screenshots and illustrations for your guides. PowerPoint, which you probably already have on your computer, works great. Try this:

- Load your screenshot into a PowerPoint slide.
- Click the Shapes tool (on the Insert tab of recent PowerPoint versions).
- From here, you can add a number of elements: boxes for instructional text, circles for numbering steps.
- Export the slide as an image—and don't forget to save the original slide so you can make changes later without starting from scratch.

Figures 4.4 and 4.11 in this chapter are examples of how the finished product can look.

Unintentional Focal Points

Most library websites and guide CMSs have focal points that we as guide authors don't design ourselves.

Navigational elements that you can't change may be built into your CMS (figure 4.8): for example, a menu bar forming a long block of color, a bold logo that appears on all pages of your site, a reference chat box, or anything else that forms an area of high contrast on the page.[12] Look over your guide design for any unintentional areas of visual focus. Consider whether you need to counter these by drawing attention with a more intentional visual focus like an image, or perhaps just use their presence on your page, acknowledge their use as focal areas, and design around them to your advantage.

Text Heavy Guide

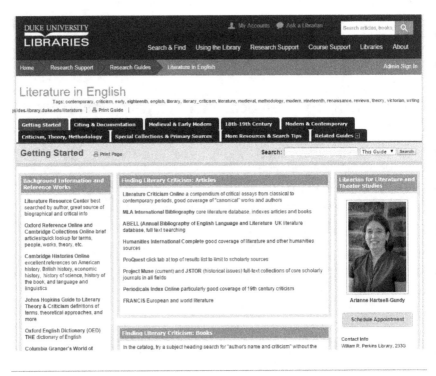

FIGURE 4.8

Contrast figure 4.7 with this guide that includes mostly text. The top navigational elements and the librarian photo on the right draw the reader's focus, and the natural tendency would probably be for the eye to go to the top left or top center of the page from there. (Arianne Hartsell-Gundy of Duke University, http://guides.library.duke.edu/literature)

Simplicity and Clarity

If you only take one idea away from this chapter, let it be this: the best way to improve readability and usability of your guide is to *simplify and clarify* the information. Less is more. "Simplicity and brevity … make [guides] very straightforward to use and understand, and also *prevents the user from being overwhelmed by myriad choices* [emphasis added]."[13]

Squint!

A simple way to check the visual design of your guide is to squint at it.

Squint your eyes until the text blurs to unreadability (or, as an alternative that would work for most librarians I know, just take your glasses off) and take a look at your guide page (figure 4.9).[14]

FIGURE 4.9

Blurring one's view of a guide page shows immediately where the high-contrast focal points are, the images at left and right. The text in the center becomes an undifferentiated gray mass; if this area contains important information then it might help to add some visual interest here.

··· **Squint! (continued)**

This forces you to stop *reading* your guide and focusing on details and get a big picture overview—it can be like taking a step back so you can look at the whole thing from a fresh angle. When the text becomes unreadable, you're forced look at the guide as a visual composition, not a textual object.

- Pay attention to where your eye is drawn first—colorful images, for example.
- How much of the guide turns into gray undifferentiated text-blobs? If it's a lot of the visible page, then there may be an intimidating amount of text that could confuse or lose your students.
- Give the page a quick skim with the F-shape principle (below) in mind to get an idea of where the reader's attention may go next: to the right and then vertically down the page.
- Is anything important hidden from view until you page down (below the fold)?

Library users are usually not willing to read through excess information to find what they need. Library websites usually "appear cluttered, overwhelming, and do not present a clear path where to begin," according to students.[15] The research guide gives us an opportunity to counteract that impression by providing them with a resource that's specific to their need—don't clutter that up too.

Remember that a good, focused guide isn't about "how to use the library," it's about how to accomplish a specific goal or succeed at a particular assignment. It shouldn't include everything on the library website. There's already a library website. Avoid overloading your students with too much information by carefully curating the information included in your guides.

Providing this sort of non-complex, non-confusing entry point to research is particularly important for novice researchers. In fact, students strongly prefer to use research guides that are structured in a simple, easy-to-follow format without too much extraneous information: a clean layout, straightforward language free of library jargon, and content that's carefully selected for relevance go farther than anything else to get students to use and appreciate library guides.[16]

Consistency of Design

One specific manifestation of simplicity and clarity is *consistency* of guide design. Using menus, visual styles, navigation, and terminology that are consistent across multiple pages and guides tacitly teaches the user how your guides work. This allows the page design and interface to recede into the background of the user's attention, which in turn helps your instructional content come to the fore.

Once the user figures out how to use a guide, the structure of the guide becomes background. It "gets out of the way" of the user and doesn't need much conscious attention, freeing up cognitive space to focus on the instructional content of the guide instead of figuring out how to navigate it or find what they need. Consistency among guides, and among pages within a guide, is a great way to help this process along: users need to figure out the organization of a page only once, not separately on every single page.

For example, college students and academic librarians are familiar with the course management system or learning management system (CMS or LMS), in which each class has its own page or set of pages. Each course or section is likely to have the same features available, just with content appropriate to the particular class—once they can navigate one class's page, the next one is easy and doesn't take any thought to figure out.

Consistency should continue across different guides too, not just within pages of the same guide. If your guides are hosted on a different server (as with LibGuides), strive to make them look as much as possible like the rest of your website.

Navigation should be visually consistent, use the same terminology, and put navigational elements in the same place on pages. Remember to use consistency in labels and text: name pages with clear labels, and use those labels when referring to other pages so students know where they are in the guide.

Consistency does not mean slavish adherence to a restrictive template or imply that one size must fit all. Just as every classroom teacher needs sufficient leeway to play to her own strengths when dealing with students, guide authors need a certain amount of flexibility to express their individual styles and expertise:

> Consistency should be, and usually is, the goal that is never achieved. Perhaps recognizability is a more useful term. A lack of it [a]ffects readability and usability.... *The*

pathfinder and its function should be clearly recognizable to anyone who has seen one before, and strict consistency will not be a critical issue or even desirable [emphasis added].[17]

The desire for consistency can simply mean that students should be able to easily find their way around the second guide they encounter after becoming comfortable with a first one. We can take advantage of the benefits of consistency with something as simple as a table of contents on the first page of each guide, a feature that users will recognize from *Wikipedia* (figure 4.10).

Wikipedia Table of Contents

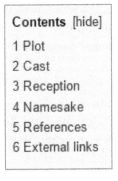

Desk Set

From Wikipedia, the free encyclopedia

Desk Set (released as **His Other Woman**
Hepburn. The screenplay was written by P

Contents [hide]

1 Plot
2 Cast
3 Reception
4 Namesake
5 References
6 External links

FIGURE 4.10

The inclusion of a simple table of contents at the top of each *Wikipedia* article provides users with a consistent and familiar navigational aid. *Wikipedia* users expect its presence without consciously thinking about it.

We're talking here about consistency in fundamental features: navigation, layout, visual design, fonts, and terminology. The content of a guide can still vary widely from other guides in your system. The goal is for students to be able to comfortably find their way around without having to stop and think.

The longer and more complex a guide, the farther it tends to depart from any given ideal of consistency. The more information and resources added to a guide, the more it tends to adopt its own individual format. That's fine as long as the essentials—navigation, structure, and so on—are still recognizable to a student using the guide, but it's another argument in favor of a simple and clear layout and carefully selected content. "Consistency facilitates ease of use if more than one pathfinder is consulted and visually unifies the publications of the library. Consistency is easier to maintain in pathfinders that are simple and direct in structure, rather than excessively hierarchical or sprawling."[18]

Striving for consistency does require collaboration and communication among guide authors, however.[19] We'll look a bit more at how to achieve this in chapter 6.

How Users Read on the Web

Readers given a printed page of text, like a book or article page, will of course tend to start at the top left and read left to right across the line, and then down the page.

What web designers know that most librarians don't is that given a *screen* of text rather than a printed page, the reader's eye seeks information in a different way. Online readers don't read a webpage start to finish like a printed page. They scan the page in a predictable way seeking the information they need, zero in on that, and quickly disregard irrelevancies.

The F Shape

User studies show that readers usually read webpages in two horizontal sweeps—across the top lines of text, then down a bit and across again—and then skim the left side of the page vertically downward. When sketched or visualized with eye-tracking software, this forms a rough F shape on the page (figure 4.11).[20]

Human-Readable URLs

It's easy to ignore the format of URLs, the actual address of a research guide. In many ways, the URL is one of the most fundamental ways in which the user interacts with your page.[*]

Whenever possible, give your guides "human-readable" URLs: an address structured so that it can convey information to the user. An eye-tracking study by Microsoft researchers indicated that searchers spent 22 to 25 percent of their search times looking at the URLs of pages in their results and that they're less likely to click on a URL that isn't easily readable.[†]

Human-readable URLs give the reader a quick navigational aid. Compare these two hypothetical addresses:

- library.edu/guides/eng101
- library.edu/page.php?pid=32447895&sid=168624

You can tell at a glance that both pages appear on a school or university library website, but the first is clearly a research guide for a first-year English class (*guides* and *eng101* cue the searcher), while the second page contains numbers that are meaningful only to the web server.

A human-readable URL is also easier to remember. An English major who has visited that first URL once can probably remember it to go back later—or if he can't remember exactly, he can start typing *eng101* into his browser and have a better chance of pulling it up from history.

Finally, they're easy for humans to convey to one another—imagine reading that second URL aloud to students in class or writing it on the board for them to copy it down accurately. Would your students even bother to try to get all those numbers right?

Unfortunately this isn't something the librarian can always control. Libraries often have content management systems that require "human-unreadable" URLs or may have a separate CMS for guides that follows a different schema of URLs. That's okay. This isn't a crucial point in guide design, but it is a useful one: if you *can* customize your guides' URLs to something friendlier, then do it!

---

[*] Andreas Bonini, 'URLs Are for People, Not Computers,' Not Implemented website, April 5, 2013, http://www.not-implemented.com/urls-are-for-people-not-computers (site now discontinued).

[†] Edward Cutrell and Zhiwei Guan, 'What Are You Looking For?' In *Proceedings of the SIGCHI Conference on Human Factors in Computing Systems* (New York: ACM, 2007), 413, doi:10.1145/1240624.1240690.

F Shaped Focal Points

FIGURE 4.11

Readers tend to read webpages in two horizontal stripes followed by skimming the page vertically. This can be influenced by adding visual focal points elsewhere on the page.

This pattern carries some implications we should keep in mind when writing research guides for the web:

- It's rare that students will read our text exhaustively start to finish. They're going to scan it, find the information they need, and ignore most other text.
- The most important information must appear in the first two paragraphs, and particularly in the first one.
- Information-carrying words should appear along that vertical bar that will be scanned: in other words, the first couple of words in each paragraph or bullet point are key. As discussed in chapter 2, make sure these are words that students will recognize, understand, and connect with their assignment.

Above the Fold

Another important consideration is the vertical length of the page. This is an incredibly simple principle: the most important information goes at the top of the page because it's most likely to be seen, and the lower on the page any given element, the less likely readers will pay attention to it.

The F shape demonstrates that most of a web user's focus stays at the top of the page. A corollary to this is that the majority of the time, readers won't scroll down the page to see what's on the next screen. The term used to describe this prime real estate, the area visible without pressing the Page Down key (figure 4.12), is *above the fold*. It's analogous to the top half of a physical newspaper: the part that's readable before the paper is picked up and unfolded.

FIGURE 4.12 LONG WEB PAGE

The shaded part of this long web page indicates how much could be below the fold on a typical monitor.

What this means to us as guide authors is that multiple, shorter, targeted pages are more advantageous—and more likely to be read—than a few long pages. For a guide page to have the largest proportion of its information seen by students, it should ideally be entirely above the fold on a typical monitor.

The information that *does* appear above the fold should be concise, skimmable, relevant and useful, and arranged for clarity so that the reader can immediately recognize it as relevant to her information need.

The user study by Hintz et al. backed up this finding: "Navigation was extremely important as three of the top ten features included the use of tabs, section headings and keeping pages to a manageable page length to limit the amount of scrolling—all pointing to common usability considerations."[21]

Unfortunately, it's likely that users will completely ignore most of our lovingly crafted "welcome to this guide" introductory text.[22] The best way to get students' attention is not to provide them with a friendly textual welcome, but to clearly present them with resources relevant to their assignment.

Writing for the Web

Since users read webpages differently from text in print, librarians need to learn how to write differently on our guides.

Fortunately for us, web authors have this figured out. There are a number of good web style guides available (for example: "Writing for the Web" on Usability.gov, http://usability.gov/how-to-and-tools/methods/writing-for-the-web.html), but here's a summary of some principles that will improve the text on your guides, making it easier for users to understand and to locate what they need.

The absolutely most important thing to remember when writing guide text is *conciseness*. Keep it brief, no matter what. Cut the word count. Don't make users filter out useless information in order to locate what they actually need. Cut the word count by half, and try to cut it by half again. (This is such a crucial tactic that I've included some more specific advice below.)

Write in a human voice, not an institutional one. Make it clear that you, the librarian-teacher, are addressing the student or user. This helps researchers feel less intimidated and reassures them that the content is relevant to their needs. "PubMed offers a greater selection of articles from major medical journals, while SciFinder Scholar has thorough coverage of studies about specific substances and reactions" is a little distant in tone and might be off-putting to an undergraduate researcher, but "Start with PubMed if you're looking for medical papers and SciFinder Scholar if you're looking for papers on certain substances or reactions" is personal and directly addresses the student and her information need.[23]

Clear labels and headers are an easy and effective tool that every web author should keep in mind at all times. Articles from the popular media site Buzzfeed remain constant viral favorites because they have eye-catching headlines with easy-to-read articles: Buzzfeed is "great at conveying information in a manner that is easily digestible to their readers. Catchy headlines with content that people actually want to read is a winning combination."[24] (Whatever opinion you might hold about Buzzfeed's content, it gets clicks.)

Clearly state the purpose of the guide, and keep the content consistent with that purpose. Label every element of the guide clearly, from the titles of pages to content headings to links, and keep the descriptions in line with the content. If they don't match, students will get confused. Users need to understand what each part the guide is for, no matter where they're looking—and remember that they may not start on your first page and read each one in turn; they may have skimmed for what they need or started on a secondary page via web search.[25]

Making Clear and Useful Links

We steer students to online databases and catalogs in almost every class we work with, so most research guides contain lots and lots of links. It's worth considering how links operate in the context of a guide and how to use links to best effect. First, some basic principles.

Links are so fundamental to the way the web works that they don't need to be explained to users. Many years ago, it was common to see web links labeled with text like Click Here, but today it's not only unnecessary, it can be counterproductive. Telling users to Click Here or Follow This Link foregrounds the interface and the action of clicking, when what you probably want is to emphasize the resource you're recommending.

Instead, make your link text informative: a specific noun is always a good choice and helps train the user to recognize what resource in particular you're recommending.[26]

Compare this:

> Click here to search for articles on your topic

With this:

> Search Academic Search Complete for articles on your topic

The second link example states what the resource is so the user will recognize it in other contexts. Users will be skimming your pages to locate what they need, your links are likely to stand out visually, and multiple linked instances of Click Here throughout the page don't provide useful or unique guideposts.

Web readers recognize links because conventionally they consist of underlined blue text, but variations on this convention are fine. Linked text may be a color other than blue, and underlines may not appear until the mouse passes over them, but the farther you depart from the blue/underline convention, the more attention the user may need to spare to identify links. Whatever convention you settle on, it's crucial that it remain consistent throughout all pages of your guide! If the users have to stop and figure out what's a link and what's not, you've put a usability barrier between them and the desired information.

This consistent convention (blue, underline) means that there's never a need to verbally indicate your links even when they appear in body text on a guide:

> When writing your literature review, start by searching Film & TV Literature Review Index for articles relevant to your topic, and you may also need to search our catalog GILFind for scholarly books. See the library's lit reviews guide for guidance on formatting and organizing. Don't forget to use proper APA style formatting as you cite your sources. Ask for help if you get stuck.

Anyone reading that paragraph on a webpage intuitively understands that the underlined phrases are links to relevant resources (it's clear in the above example even without blue text). There's no need to break up the concise instructions with Click Here or Follow This Link to …. Each phrase clearly indicates where the link will go, and the one phrase ("Ask for help") that doesn't name or describe a specific resource obviously goes to either a contact page or a librarian's e-mail address.

Novice guide authors sometimes even spell out URLs in text: "Use the library's catalog at http://gilfind.gsu.edu to find books." Never do this on a webpage—visible URLs are ugly and break the flow of text. The reader can get the URL by mousing over the link if needed. Revise those instructions to something like this: "Use the library's catalog to find books." That's much more readable, and the link is still clear.

Annotating Links

Most of the above advice applies to links that appear within regular text, but another common practice in research guides is providing users with a list of useful database links with annotations to help users select resources. This is such a common guide feature that it deserves some special attention.

Conciseness is always key, and that goes for list length as well. Offer links to the key databases or sites that will really be useful for a particular information need, and resist the urge to link to everything that *might* be useful. A list of three databases gives students a clear path to start their research; a list of fifteen is likely to intimidate them and leave them not knowing where to start.

Annotated database links can be one of the most useful features of a guide when done well. When done badly, they can confuse students and discourage them from using your guide. (Of course, this goes for annotations when linking to any kind of site—I'm using *databases* here as shorthand since it's probably the most common type of resource we link to.)

Database Annotations

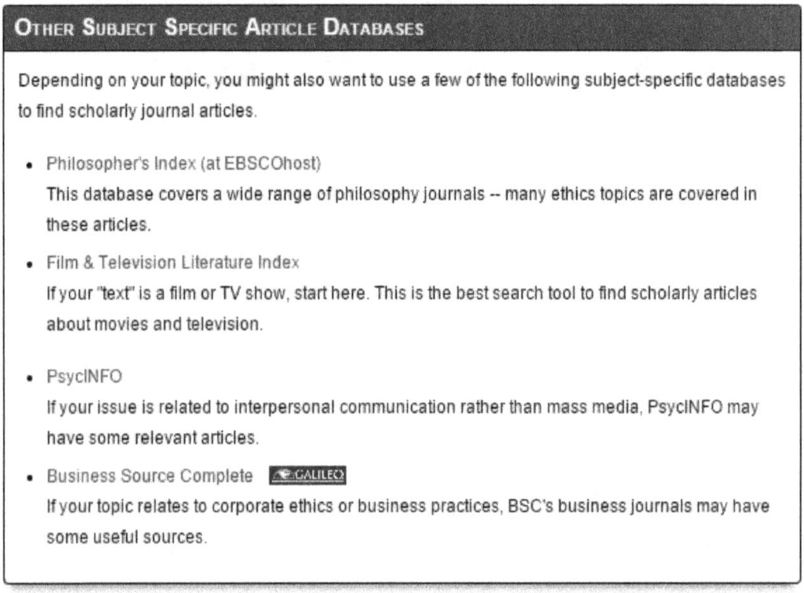

> **OTHER SUBJECT SPECIFIC ARTICLE DATABASES**
>
> Depending on your topic, you might also want to use a few of the following subject-specific databases to find scholarly journal articles.
>
> - Philosopher's Index (at EBSCOhost)
>   This database covers a wide range of philosophy journals -- many ethics topics are covered in these articles.
> - Film & Television Literature Index
>   If your "text" is a film or TV show, start here. This is the best search tool to find scholarly articles about movies and television.
> - PsycINFO
>   If your issue is related to interpersonal communication rather than mass media, PsycINFO may have some relevant articles.
> - Business Source Complete   [GALILEO]
>   If your topic relates to corporate ethics or business practices, BSC's business journals may have some useful sources.

FIGURE 4.13

Annotate links with concise information relevant to the guide objectives.

Keep annotations brief. Brevity results in clarity and good web readability; too-long text discourages the user (figure 4.13). One study of research guide use found that "short annotations describing resources were highly desirable.... Students are not willing to read an annotation more than a sentence or two long."[27]

Don't regurgitate marketing copy. Guides often include database descriptions and other text that has been written by one of our vendors and copied and pasted by the librarian. Look at this example:

> Containing fully searchable text for more than 250 of the world's most respected phrenology journals, Database One represents a partnership between INFOCO and Globex to bring the Index of Critical Studies and the UltraBibliography of the New Education Society Online, as well as over 150 monographs, together in a comprehensive digital format for the first time.

That's comparable to annotations appearing in many research guides and contains a composite of actual wording (real product and vendor names redacted) from several of my library's database descriptions. Not only is text like this more advertisement than anything else, it's also written for the vendor's library customers, not for students, and it's full of baffling jargon that would scare off a novice researcher.

Crafting a useful annotation for a database takes a little effort, but it's worth it to the readability of your page. Look at your guide from the perspective of a student and compare the blurb above with something like this:

> This database is a good starting point to find articles for your case study paper. Make sure to check the "peer-reviewed" box when you search so that you get only scholarly sources.

That's much clearer, much friendlier, and written directly to the student's needs instead of sounding like it's trying to sell a subscription.

Keep instructions to a minimum. Most users will click through to a link without reading annotations carefully, so if you're including any instructions or tips, keep them very brief or they'll be lost. Don't explain anything that will be clear to the user after they click through; it's wasted space. Tell them only what they need to know before they click, like the above example alerting them to the peer-review check box.[28]

What to Cut?

Earlier I said to cut your word count by half and then half again. Cutting text by 75 percent may be a startling recommendation at first. We often craft our instructions with such meticulous care that it is hard to imagine jettisoning three quarters of it. How should you approach editing your text down by such a large amount? This isn't as hard as it sounds, and there are plenty of ways to do it.

Eliminate long introductions. Many guides include paragraphs of text explaining the purpose of the guide and describing what students will find on it. You can usually dispense with this. Not only are large chunks of text less readable on a screen than on the page, it's more likely that users will simply ignore introductory text, particularly if it's long.[29] Make the purpose of the page clear—which you may be able to do simply with a good title and clear page headings—and leave it at that.

Use librarian jargon judiciously. There are many terms that we use as part of our professional vocabulary without a second thought that cause students to come to a screeching halt in their comprehension. Get rid of terms like *catalog record, OPAC, holdings,* and anything else the slightest bit jargony.

On the other hand, there are legitimate cases in which students really need to learn a library term, either because a clearer synonym doesn't exist or because they'll be encountering it frequently in their work (like *abstract, database,* or *peer-reviewed*), in which case define it once—clearly and concisely, in a place they won't miss. Don't shy away from using research terminology if it's necessary, just be aware of what terms are useful and what's confusing.

Good practice with terminology use tends to happen naturally with concise writing anyway. Generally speaking, the longer and wordier a guide is, the more likely it is to include unnecessary or confusing jargon. Keeping your text focused and concise will usually help keep confusing terminology to a minimum and ensure good readability.[30]

Keep it simple, keep it focused. Cut anything that's just "nice to have" or inessential. Remember, when in doubt leave it out. The library already has a website and your guide doesn't have to be it.

The ideas about learning objectives from chapter 2 help with this. If the guide is tailored to a learning objective, focus is much easier to achieve, and you have a clear guideline to help decide what material to cut and what to keep.

Break up long sentences and paragraphs. Reformat long paragraphs into scannable bulleted lists. Cut extraneous words and focus on keywords and trigger words that direct readers to the information they need to complete a task.

Eliminate redundancy. If your text is clear and includes appropriate keywords that users recognize, don't repeat yourself. If your audience is less experienced students, you may need to reinforce text with images or vice versa, but if the guide is targeted at more advanced researchers like grad students or faculty, one or the other probably suffices.

Cut passive voice. This makes your text clearer and easier to follow, as well as simply shorter.

Brevity and clarity of focus help keep guides accessible and easy to use. The longer the guide, the more complex it becomes and the more it moves away from the role of clearly introducing students to research resources.[31]

Example

Figures 4.14 and 4.15 are an example of how I've applied a few of the ideas from this chapter and previous ones to improve a course guide I use frequently.[32] This is a journalism ethics class tasked with writing a paper that includes a literature review section followed by discussion of a real-world case study.

Some of the changes I made:

- Radically reducing the amount of text on the page. I cut the "library basics" section entirely. This is something I used to include on all my guides, but while it contains useful information, it's not always applicable to every assignment and I'd rather focus the guides more specifically than include potentially irrelevant information. My contact information was already there on the right, so that part of the "basics" section was redundant anyway.
- Getting rid of the "start here" page and making the first page one that jumped straight into the first part of the assignment. I could even remove this page or move it, since the class has often already chosen topics and is at the lit review stage of the assignment by the time they meet me and see the guide.

Research Guide (Before)

Jour 4800: Media Ethics & Society (old version): Start Here

FIGURE 4.14

First page of the Journalism 4800 guide before revisions. It's got much more text on the home page and is structured more by source format (a books page and an articles page) than around the assignment.

Research Guide (After)

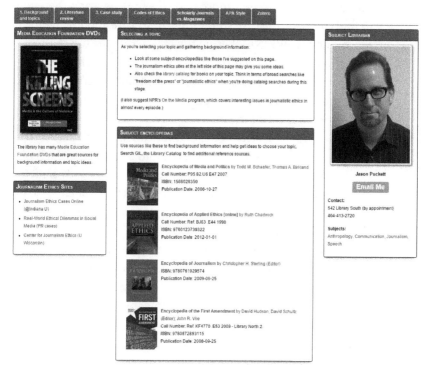

FIGURE 4.15

After some revising, the text has been re-chunked and moved to later pages, and the guide is structured more closely to the parts of the assignment. Images add some visual interest, and the overall guide is more readable.

- Improving organization to follow the assignment more clearly. The old guide was organized at least partly around the format of the sources—books and articles—while students are more interested in how to find sources for the lit review and then how to find them for the case study. They don't care about what form those sources take. Numbering the tabs across the top of the guide helps make it clear that these are intended to help with discrete stages of the assignment. Students also don't have to go back and forth as much between instructions on the first page and resource links on the interior pages.

- Reorganizing the instructional text for conciseness. I didn't actually delete much text, just moved it to later pages. Much of the instructional content on the old version was already bulleted and scannable, which is good, but I felt it was too much all in one place. I chunked it better so that each stage of the assignment has its own concise instructions on the relevant page.

- Adding some visual interest with cover images. It's a small thing, but the book cover images will help draw the student's eye down the page to the resources I'm recommending. This is particularly useful since the page goes below the fold: by drawing attention further down the page, I make it more likely that students will notice that the recommendations continue below the first screen.

Is it perfect? Of course not. But I think it's better, according to several of the principles we've been examining, and when I go back and compare the two versions from a student's perspective, the revised one seems clearer and easier to follow. Every guide is a work in progress, and I continue to informally assess and adjust it bit by bit, each semester I work with the class.

Summing Up: Some Simple Best Practices

Designing and writing a good research guide is all about clarity and simplicity.

- Conciseness and focus are key. Keep the guide small in every way possible: visually, textually, and in its topical scope. Reduce clutter and eliminate unnecessary information.
- Visual appearance has a real effect on how effective your instruc-

tional content will be. Neat, clean design has a positive impact on the information contained in your guides.

- Images (and other high-contrast elements) can serve as focal points to draw users' eye to key elements and important information and help reinforce the message of the text.
- Consistent design across pages and guides helps users concentrate on the information and spend less time trying to find their way around your site.
- Make your text brief. Cut it by half and by half again if you can. Users will typically skim for the information they need rather than reading word for word. The less text there is on the page, the more likely it will be read. Keep it short and avoid jargon.
- Make your linked words informative rather than using Click Here. Use the standard convention of underlined, colored text to make your links clear. Annotate your links with relevant information, not vendor marketing copy.

Above all, keep your audience in mind and be prepared to look at your guide with fresh eyes. Try to think like a student, not like a librarian—give them enough information for what they need to accomplish and nothing to detract from that goal.

Notes

1. Aaron Schmidt and Amanda Etches, *User Experience (UX) Design for Libraries* (Chicago: ALA TechSource, 2012), 4–5.
2. William Hemmig, "Online Pathfinders," *Reference Services Review* 33, no. 1 (February 2005): 70–71, doi:10.1108/00907320510581397.
3. Jim M. Kapoun, "Re-thinking the Library Pathfinder," *College & Undergraduate Libraries* 2, no. 1 (1995): 95.
4. Lori S. Mestre, *Designing Effective Library Tutorials* (Oxford: Chandos, 2012), 107.
5. Candice Dahl, "Electronic Pathfinders in Academic Libraries," *College & Research Libraries* 62, no 3 (2001): 234.
6. Nancy H. Dewald, "Transporting Good Library Instruction Practices into the Web Environment," *Journal of Academic Librarianship* 25, no. 1 (January 1999): 30, doi:10.1016/S0099-1333(99)80172-4.
7. Hemmig, "Online Pathfinders," 67.

8. Nedda Ahmed, "Design," in *Using LibGuides to Enhance Library Services*, ed. Aaron W. Dobbs, Ryan L. Sittler, and Douglas Cook (Chicago: ALA Tech-Source, 2013), 104.

9. Kimberley Hintz et al., "Letting Students Take the Lead," *Evidence Based Library and Information Practice* 5, no. 4 (2010): 45.

10. Lori S. Mestre, "Student Preference for Tutorial Design," *Reference Services Review* 40, no. 2 (May 2012): 269, doi:10.1108/00907321211228318.

11. Ibid., 271–72.

12. Ahmed, "Design," 107.

13. Dahl, "Electronic Pathfinders in Academic Libraries," 232–33.

14. Ahmed, "Design," 107.

15. Caroline Sinkinson et al., "Guiding Design," *portal: Libraries & the Academy* 12, no. 1 (January 2012): 77.

16. Hintz et al., "Letting Students Take the Lead," 47.

17. Hemmig, "Online Pathfinders," 77.

18. Dahl, "Electronic Pathfinders in Academic Libraries," 231.

19. Ahmed, "Design," 109.

20. Jakob Nielsen, "F-Shaped Pattern for Reading Web Content," Nielsen Norman Group, April 17, 2006, http://www.nngroup.com/articles/f-shaped-pattern-reading-web-content.

21. Hintz et al., "Letting Students Take the Lead," 45.

22. Mestre, *Designing Effective Library Tutorials*, 115.

23. Jackie Werner, "CHEM 4000—Fundamentals of Chemical Analysis," Georgia State University Research Guides, accessed April 3, 2015, http://research.library.gsu.edu/c.php?g=115758&p=752527.

24. Anne Marie Suchanek, "How Buzzfeed Is Taking Over the Internet," *Information Space* (blog), Syracuse University School of Information Studies, January 21, 2014, http://infospace.ischool.syr.edu/2014/01/21/how-buzzfeed-is-taking-over-the-internet.

25. Sinkinson et al., "Guiding Design," 80.

26. "anthony," "Why Your Links Should Never Say 'Click Here,'" *UX Movement* (blog), June 20, 2012, http://uxmovement.com/content/why-your-links-should-never-say-click-here.

27. Hintz et al., "Letting Students Take the Lead," 46.

28. Ahmed, "Design," 112.

29. Mestre, *Designing Effective Library Tutorials*, 115.

30. Dahl, "Electronic Pathfinders in Academic Libraries," 235.

31. Ibid., 72.

32. Old version: research.library.gsu.edu/c.php?g=115485; current version: research.library.gsu.edu/jour4800.

References

Ahmed, Nedda. "Design: Why It Is Important and How to Get It Right." In *Using LibGuides to Enhance Library Services: A LITA Guide*, edited by Aaron W. Dobbs, Ryan L. Sittler, and Douglas Cook, 103–19. Chicago: ALA TechSource, an imprint of the American Library Association, 2013.

"anthony." "Why Your Links Should Never Say 'Click Here.'" *UX Movement* (blog), June 20, 2012. http://uxmovement.com/content/why-your-links-should-never-say-click-here.

Bonini, Andreas. "URLs Are for People, Not Computers." Not Implemented website, April 5, 2013. http://www.not-implemented.com/urls-are-for-people-not-computers (site now discontinued).

Cutrell, Edward, and Zhiwei Guan. "What Are You Looking For? An Eye-Tracking Study of Information Usage in Web Search." In *Proceedings of the SIGCHI Conference on Human Factors in Computing Systems*, 407–16. New York: ACM, 2007. doi:10.1145/1240624.1240690.

Dahl, Candice. "Electronic Pathfinders in Academic Libraries: An Analysis of Their Content and Form." *College & Research Libraries* 62, no. 3 (2001): 227–37.

Dewald, Nancy H. "Transporting Good Library Instruction Practices into the Web Environment: An Analysis of Online Tutorials." *Journal of Academic Librarianship* 25, no. 1 (January 1999): 26–31. doi:10.1016/S0099-1333(99)80172-4.

Hemmig, William. "Online Pathfinders: Toward an Experience-Centered Model." *Reference Services Review* 33, no. 1 (February 2005): 66–87. doi:10.1108/00907320510581397.

Hintz, Kimberley, Paula Farrar, Shirin Eshghi, Barbara Sobol, Jo-Anne Naslund, Teresa Lee, Tara Stephens, and Aleha McCauley. "Letting Students Take the Lead: A User-Centred Approach to Evaluating Subject Guides." *Evidence Based Library and Information Practice* 5, no. 4 (2010): 39–52.

Kapoun, Jim M. "Re-thinking the Library Pathfinder." *College & Undergraduate Libraries* 2, no. 1 (1995): 93–105.

Mestre, Lori S. *Designing Effective Library Tutorials: A Guide for Accommodating Multiple Learning Styles.* Oxford: Chandos, 2012.

———. "Student Preference for Tutorial Design: A Usability Study." *Reference Services Review* 40, no. 2 (May 2012): 258–76. doi:10.1108/00907321211228318.

Nielsen, Jakob. "F-Shaped Pattern for Reading Web Content." Nielsen Norman Group, April 17, 2006. http://www.nngroup.com/articles/f-shaped-pattern-reading-web-content.

Schmidt, Aaron, and Amanda Etches. *User Experience (UX) Design for Libraries.* Chicago: ALA TechSource, an imprint of the American Library Association, 2012.

Sinkinson, Caroline, Stephanie Alexander, Alison Hicks, and Meredith Kahn. "Guiding Design: Exposing Librarian and Student Mental Models of Research Guides." *portal: Libraries & the Academy* 12, no. 1 (January 2012): 63–84.

Suchanek, Anne Marie. "How Buzzfeed Is Taking Over the Internet." *Information Space* (blog), Syracuse University School of Information Studies, January 21, 2014. http://infospace.ischool.syr.edu/2014/01/21/how-buzzfeed-is-taking-over-the-internet.

Werner, Jackie. "CHEM 4000—Fundamentals of Chemical Analysis: Using Web of Science." Georgia State University Research Guides. Accessed April 3, 2015. http://research.library.gsu.edu/c.php?g=115758&p=752527.

CHAPTER 5

Assessment

WE PUT A LOT of work into our guides. How do we know whether that work is worthwhile, and whether these guides are actually useful? And what do we mean by "useful," exactly?

Assessment allows librarians to determine whether guides are meeting the needs of the library and its goals and the needs of the users. There are a number of ways to do this, with a wide range of complexity and effort involved, but it doesn't have to be a difficult process.

Assessment can be simple. It boils down to

- Decide *what needs* the guide should fulfill.
- Determine *how to measure* whether, or to what extent, the guide meets those needs.
- Gather information that will tell you *how well* the guide is succeeding at those goals.

What Are You Assessing?

What do you need to know about your guides? Whether they're helping students achieve the aims of an assignment? Whether users like using them and will continue to do so? Whether they are getting enough hits to justify the cost to the institution?

These are all valid questions, and there are many possibilities for what you may need to know about your guides and how your learners use them. By first defining your assessment needs as specifically as you can, you'll make planning assessment much easier on yourself.

Some of these questions take more effort to answer than others. Some can be answered simply by gathering data or generating reports from your web server. Some require reaching out to users more actively to ask them for their opinions or collaborating with teaching faculty to have students engage in an assessment exercise. The goals of your assessment will suggest the tools and methods you may need to use. For example:

- *Do your users find the guides helpful and easy to use? Would your users return to your guides for help in the future?* Questions like these are subjective and perception-based. They will give you an idea of how successful your UX design is and possibly some sense of how useful your guides' learning objectives are to students. Some form of user survey or focus group would answer these.

- *Are your users actually achieving the guides' learning objectives?* This is related to the previous questions, but a bit different. This is actually something you'd measure objectively through observation: do students understand what you're trying to teach them, and can they accomplish something after consulting the guide that they couldn't before? Can we tell if they learned? This might best fit a course- or assignment-oriented guide, and a quiz is a good way to measure it, ideally involving collaboration from the course instructor.

- *Are your guides actually being seen and used?* If guides are buried several clicks deep on the library site, they might not be getting the traffic you want, especially if you're investing many librarian hours and thousands of dollars per year into your guide system. This type of assessment can probably be conducted with an analysis of web server logs, using either your site's existing logs, the built-in analytics in a system like LibGuides, or a third-party application like Google Analytics.

- *Do your guides meet your library's defined standards?* This assumes that you have some standards defined, of course. There are many possible things you may want to assess here: self-defined quality standards, usability or design standards, or accessibility standards for disabled users, for example. Assessment like this would need a rubric of some sort and probably requires analysis of the relevant guides by an individual librarian or a committee.

The focus of your assessment may be chosen based on a number of factors. Assessment can help provide justification for the cost of a guide system or validate a pilot guide project. It may endorse the effectiveness of guides as an instructional tool, evaluate the success of a marketing campaign to promote guides to users, or test the applicability of library learning outcomes to a particular course.

In this chapter we'll examine a few useful and common assessment tools and look briefly at how each might be applied to research guides. You and your colleagues have designed, written, and implemented your guides, and you'll have the clearest insights into how best to adapt these ideas to fit your own institution. The reference list at the end of the chapter contains many more sources by library assessment experts.

Using Rubrics and Analyzing Guide Content

How to Use Rubrics

A rubric is simply a set of criteria for defining the standards by which an item (a research guide, in this case) is to be assessed and judged.

An assessment rubric provides a way for librarians to take subjective questions about a guide—quality, usability, scope, and so on—and put them into a more objective framework to help with analysis and comparison. Rubrics are useful in several ways: they define and constrain the specific questions being assessed so that assessment doesn't just diffuse into vague ratings of *good/bad*, they provide a means for several members of an assessment group to evaluate based on the same criteria, and they can provide a way to quantify assessment for later analysis.

If you haven't yet defined the specific assessment questions you want to answer, start with some broad aspects of your guides that you want to examine, like visual design, instructional quality, ease of use, currency of information, or accessibility for disabled users. These areas could be defined by a single librarian, decided at a department level, based on institutional goals or projects, or some combination.

From there it becomes easier to define specific criteria that indicate whether a guide meets those standards. In their finished form, these criteria should ultimately be items that a librarian looking at the guide could identify and rate in some way, whether that rating is a simple *true/false*, a count of how often an item occurs on a guide, a numeric scale, or some other method. As always, keep the user's perspective in mind. It makes defining assessment criteria easier!

If ease of use is a desired area of assessment, for example, your rubric might include items like how many clicks does it take to reach the guide from the library's homepage, how easy is it to spot a particular item on a guide page, whether the guide includes jargon unclear to students, or whether the guide includes a clear explanation of its purpose.

If the library is assessing instructional quality of guides, the rubric might examine whether learning objectives are clearly defined, how well the guide addresses a specific course assignment, the clarity and specificity of database link annotations, or how well the guide addresses multiple learning styles.

Note that these questions can be a mix of objective (how many clicks, is this link broken, does this item appear on the guide) and subjective (how difficult, how attractive, what constitutes library jargon). That's okay—the point of the rubric is to give the reviewing librarian a framework in which to exercise her judgment and to focus that judgment on relevant areas, not to eliminate her judgment from the equation.

Assessment Example: Rubric

A librarian wishes to assess a series of research guides to evaluate them for clarity and readability. He will have a couple of colleagues work with him on the assessment project, and they will ultimately produce a summary report for the reference department to present to library administration. He designs a rubric to keep everyone on the same page with what they're assessing.

Having read chapter 4 of this book and supplemented it with some ideas from usability studies and after discussion with colleagues about what they all want from their research guides, he settles on the following questions as a rough draft:

1. Is the text on this guide clear and readable by students?
    a. Are there long blocks of text present that should be broken up or edited down?
    b. Is any included library jargon necessary, and are terms defined where needed?
2. Is it clear what the guide is useful for, and is it easy to find important information quickly?

a. Are the guide's objectives stated (implicitly or explicitly) up front?
b. Is there information on the guide extraneous to these objectives?
c. Is there important or useful information "below the fold" on a standard monitor?
3. Are links to databases and other resources presented well?
   a. Are link annotations free of marketing-style copy?
   b. Is it clear how students might use a given resource in the context of the assignment or research objective?
   c. Are too many resources and links presented, potentially confusing researchers?

To keep things simple and consistent, he puts all this into a rubric format with each item to be given a score from 1 to 5, "strongly disagree" to "strongly agree," rephrasing items where needed since some of the questions in the initial draft are phrased so that an "agree" indicates an undesirable situation.

The final rubric looks like figure 5.1. A "perfect" guide would have a total score of 40 points by this yardstick. The project leader sets up a Google form for the assessment team to use so that he won't have to do manual data entry later.

From here, the assessment committee could take a number of approaches, depending on how much time and effort they can put into the assessment project. They could divide the number of guides by three and assign them among themselves, either randomly or based on subject expertise. Or all three assessors could review all guides—the numbers would not be redundant since they're just providing additional opinions about each guide. Or they could take a middle ground, assigning themselves enough guides to review so that every guide has at least two assessment scores tallied.

The scores will be downloaded to Excel to clean up into a final version and accompanied by a short written report for the department, and naturally the assessors will delete any identifying information about who reviewed what guides. Based on the results, the department might decide to take some training on web usability or establish some new best practices, or individual guide authors may decide to go back and edit some their guides—or the librarians may decide that this aspect of their guides is in good shape for this year and move on to another project.

Sample Assessment Rubric

Numeric score:
1=Strongly disagree
5=Strongly agree

1. Readability

a. Text is concise and readable with no long paragraphs

b. Text is free of library jargon, terms are defined as needed

Readability total: _____

2. Clarity

a. Guide's objectives are clear

b. No extraneous information on guide

c. Important information above the fold

Clarity total: _____

3. Links and resources

a. Annotations free of vendor marketing copy

b. Resources annotated to aid their use in the guide's objectives

c. Will not confuse students with too many options

Resources total: _____

Guide total: _____

FIGURE 5.1

This rubric takes some subjective questions of judgment and quantifies them in a way that makes it easier to assess guides against a defined standard.

When embarking on an assessment project like this, remember to look at what other libraries have done and build on published rubrics for your own library's needs. For some good example rubrics for a variety of purposes, look at works from this chapter's references.[1]

User Surveys

How to Use Surveys

Surveys are one of the most popular methods of assessment in libraries.[2] Surveys combine the ease of online access and automated data collection of web analytics with a measure of active feedback that allows library users to share their input.

Obviously, a survey or poll helps if you need feedback from your users—not quantitative data or objective analysis of guides, but opinion and input (though of course you may wish to quantify and analyze survey results to see the final picture).

Surveys may be directed to an audience of students, faculty, or both and are a means of encouraging those who use your guides to report back on how the guides suit their needs, what's working, what's missing, and suggestions for improvement.

One advantage of a survey is the ability to embed it into the guide itself, where it's visible to those actually using the guide for research. Guide CMSs like LibGuides may include a basic survey or feedback form built in to the system, but these built-in tools may sometimes be too simplistic and lack some desirable features. For example, the LibGuides poll systems collect response data only in a simple form viewable on the guide or e-mailed individually to the guide owner, requiring manual entry into a spreadsheet for analysis.

It's often practical to use a dedicated survey system that captures data directly to an online spreadsheet since this can export directly to Excel or a Google spreadsheet so you can easily analyze and share the results. Google Forms works well for this (and costs nothing); the survey can be provided as a link or actually embedded in a usable form in the page. Plenty of other online tools like SurveyMonkey are available and work equally well.

The length of the survey is up to you, depending on what you need to determine. Remember that "survey fatigue"—too many surveys and too many questions—dulls users' interest and makes it less likely that they'll complete the survey. Use the same principles you learned in earlier chapters: keep questions concise and focused on what you really need to know, and don't include extraneous "it would be nice to know" questions. Short surveys get more responses.

Multiple-choice, *true/false,* and *yes/no* questions—anything that can be answered with a mouse click rather than a written response—also tend to get more responses and are easier to tabulate in spreadsheet and graph form when reporting out your results. Survey responses like this can usually be compiled, analyzed, and turned into data automatically, which is useful for a one-person assessment project.

On the other hand, open answers and comment fields that allow free text entry provide users the opportunity to surprise you with insights about issues you hadn't anticipated. Subjective answers like these can't always be easily quantified and put into a spreadsheet and will always require a human to read, consider, and analyze them. The tradeoff in effort may often be worth it, even for an assessment team of one, though, since it gives the user the chance to offer direct feedback on the guides. Courtois, Higgins, and Kapur designed an extraordinarily simple assessment instrument with a single question: "Was this guide helpful to you?" accompanied by Likert scale rating button and a comment box for users to enter text.[3]

It's possible to be highly specific in targeting the audience for an assessment instrument. For example, if you want to be certain that all respondents are from a specific section of a course, activate the survey the day of the instruction session for that class and have them work through it during class, or share the URL only via the course's learning management system site. It may be possible to require a password or otherwise restrict access to a survey, but do this sparingly: minimizing entry barriers will help your response rate.

Library assessment often seems to default to asking users "Was this (guide, class, or service) useful?" which may not always be what we're really after. Students may feel a guide was useful (or at least be willing to click *yes* if asked), but many cases the pertinent questions are not about students' feelings. True assessment questions probably have more to do with whether it's an effective teaching tool: questions like "Which of these is a primary source?" or "What is the call number of this book?" Asking students questions that measure learning outcomes may be more practical and will give you a better picture of how and whether the guide is helping them learn. (Courtois et al. *were* specifically seeking user opinions rather than attempting to measure student learning in the assessment project mentioned above.)

Assessment Examples: Surveys

Dalton and Pan conducted an assessment project on their LibGuides pilot that included a combination of quantitative usage data from web analytics (see below) and qualitative survey data. They determined that student feedback would be a key element in establishing whether the pilot was successful. They presented students with a short three-question survey asking

- whether they had heard of or used the guides
- how they would rate guides on a scale of 1–10
- which feature they found most helpful or would like to see added to the guides.[4]

The survey is short enough to encourage participation by busy students and focused to give librarians the specific feedback they need: whether students are using the guides (also informed by the results of their web analytics numbers), a general overall opinion about their quality in a simple numeric form, and comments that can help librarians decide on future directions for guide development.

Mahaffy used a similar user survey to discover student opinions about a particular assignment-focused guide, comparing responses to a paper-based guide with a comparable online version.[5] In addition to questions similar to Dalton and Pan's, she also asked "Were you satisfied with the research you gathered for the assignment?" Comparing responses from two versions of a guide—paper and electronic, in this case, but two versions of an online guide are feasible as well—could enable the librarian to identify useful aspects of each iteration and adapt them for the next version of a guide.

I used an even more outcome-focused, quiz-style survey for students in a research-intensive journalism history course to establish how well my guide was helping students achieve the research necessary for the assignment.[6] Each of these questions had multiple choice answers that could, hopefully, be answered based on information present in the guide:

- What sources could you use to identify useful historic newspaper articles?
- Which of these might be a primary source for a Jour 4040 paper on press coverage of the Civil War?
- Once you've identified historic newspaper articles, what tools could you use to locate the actual newspapers?
- Secondary sources are useful for this paper because:

a. They were written by those present at the time of the historic events
b. They can provide background and historical context not present in primary sources
c. They include citations to primary sources in their bibliographies

Based on the results of the assessment, I was able to tell that students had no problem distinguishing primary and secondary sources and identifying these sources' different roles in the research paper but that they still had difficulty actually locating the newspapers they needed. I revised that section the guide to provide more detailed information and step-by-step instructions (and also began emphasizing that stage of the process during in-person class sessions).

Web Analytics

Web analytics tools are anything that allows the librarian to view data on how users are accessing the website. Since research guides are just webpages, analyzing your web traffic can be an effective and straightforward way to answer some types of assessment questions. Because you're working with automatically generated data, assessment of web analytics has some advantages: it isn't dependent on convincing busy users to take time to participate, and the analysis can generally be done by a single librarian. (Depending on the technology available to you, you may need to consult with your web librarian to collect the data, however.)

A detailed discussion of web analytics technology is beyond the scope of this book, but we'll look briefly at the possibilities.

Web analytics can answer questions like

- How much are our guides used overall? Which types of guides are used more than others?
- Where are users finding links to our guides? Does linking from our learning management system (LMS) significantly increase student use of a course guide?
- How much are guides used before, during, and after the library instruction session for the related course? Does an instruction session have a significant impact on guide usage?
- Do our online students use guides more than on-campus users? Are they using different types of guides?

- How often do students follow links from guides to get to our databases and catalog?

Web analytics are good for providing quantitative data about guide use: when, where, for how long, how much, and so on. They are much less useful for more qualitative-based questions relevant to user experience or student learning.

Typically, you'll have three general options for gathering web analytics:

- If your research guides are hosted on your library's web server, there should be web logs that can be downloaded and analyzed. You will probably need to isolate a specific subset of logs to limit your analysis just to your research guides. Obviously the specifics will depend on your library's setup, so talk to your web librarian.
- A dedicated guide-specific content management system (CMS) like LibGuides has built-in analytics features (figure 5.2) that can generate many basic statistical reports and may be able to download data in a format like Excel for easier manipulation.

LibGuides Statistics

FIGURE 5.2

LibGuides provides basic guide analytics that are sufficient for many assessment purposes: hits to guides (or sets of guides) across a given date range, basically. More detailed analysis may require additional software.

- If your system doesn't track the data you need, you may want to consider supplementing it with a third-party application like Google Analytics (http://google.com/analytics; see figure 5.3). Google Analytics is free and easy to set up (it requires a snippet of code to be added to your site) and tracks a great deal of additional information like length of time spent on the site, user demographics, mobile usage, search terms used on the site, users' paths as they navigate through the guides, and more. Obviously this is something you'd need to set up *before* the time period to be assessed; Google Analytics can't track data retroactively.

Google Analytics Sample

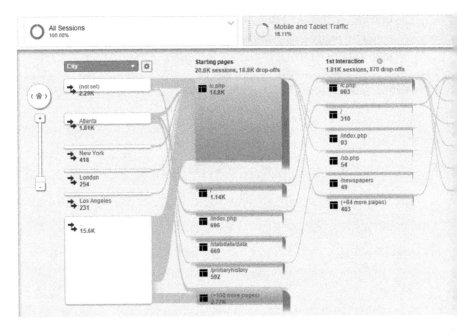

FIGURE 5.3

Google Analytics provides highly detailed options for viewing guide use information—in this case, users' locations and use of mobile devices and tablets are combined with a report on their paths navigating through the guide site.

What Analytics Assessment Can Tell You

The most basic form of web analytics involves simply tracking the number of guide views. The most fundamental assessment question may be "Are people viewing our guides?" Comparing the number of times your guides have been accessed with the number of students enrolled may well be enough to give you a "good enough" ballpark answer for your purposes.

More specific assessment questions that a view count can answer might include

- Comparing the amount of traffic to guides in a specific subject area with enrollment in that subject's courses can give you an idea of whether some disciplines use guides more heavily than others.
- Comparing the number of guide views before and after a publicity effort—featuring them on your library's blog, having instruction librarians promote them in classes, or adding a prominent link on your home page—can give you an idea how successful your "marketing" has been and give you an idea how to improve guide use in the future.

Deeper or more detailed analysis of traffic can sometimes give more insights, often requiring some interpretation. For example:

- Tracking the number of new visitors versus returning visitors may be one indicator of whether students are finding the guides useful. Return visits could indicate that students are bookmarking guides for later reference. A one-time hit might indicate that a visitor looked at the guide and decided that it wasn't what they needed (or might indicate that they found a desired resource and moved on successfully without the need to return to the guide).
- Examining referral traffic gives information about how your users are finding guides: via search engines, links from your homepage, a direct link from within the LMS page for a course, from other pages on your institution's site external to the library, from your social media profiles, or outside sites. (This can sometimes lead to discovering that your guides are linked from unexpected places!)
- Tracking the amount of time spent on guides can indicate something about how students are using them (figure 5.4). A short average time may show that students are finding them and deciding not to use them (if they go on to an unrelated page or a search engine)

or that they're using them as a quick jumping-off point for database links. Longer use could show that students are taking time to read your instructional materials and view tutorials (and don't forget to check YouTube view statistics for your video tutorials as well).

History Buttons

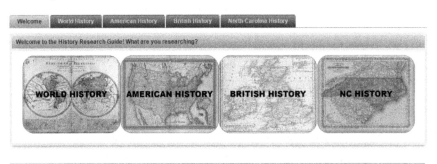

FIGURE 5.4

Analytics assessment revealed that students were finding this history guide's front page but were ignoring the tabs and not clicking through to later pages. The librarian created these large buttons to draw students' attention to the interior pages. (Heidi Buchanan, Western Carolina University, http://researchguides.wcu.edu/History)

All of the above data can be gathered via Google Analytics. Don't forget that it's usually possible to compare subsets of guides with one another—guides for specific subjects or courses, the same guides at different times of the year—or comparisons from the same point in different semesters can be put side-by-side to examine whether the guides are being used differently or to track changes in usage. Your web librarian can advise you on other possibilities for information available from your specific setup.

Assessment Examples: Analytics

Baldwin and McFadden suggest tracking the number of unique page views and return visits for a specific course guide and comparing it with the number of students in the class, with one to five page views per student and one to three return visits in the six-month period following library instruction serving as their target numbers.[7] This was part of a project combining web analytics with a rubric to clarify the value of their LibGuides in a number of contexts: economic, instructional, distance education, and incidental. While it sounds like an assessment project this ambitious would require extensive user surveys and labor-intensive content analysis, they were able to create a report analyzing all these areas (and identifying areas needing additional effort) based on web analytics data.

An instruction librarian is assessing the most effective means of increasing guide traffic, comparing linking from the course's LMS page, promoting a guide in class, and e-mailing the URL to students after class. She is working with three sections of a course, and instead of using the same guide for all sections, she duplicates the guide so she can track hits separately for the three classes. Since the guide for each section of the course has a unique URL, this is easy to analyze: define the time period, pull a report for each guide, adjust for class size, and compare numbers.

Durrant conducted an assessment of Indiana University-Purdue University Indianapolis's research guides with the postulate that the "successful" use of a guide involved a student either proceeding to an electronic resource, using instructional materials, or requesting help from a librarian. Google Analytics allowed her to track how frequently these events took place during a student's visit to a guide in her designated pool. Additional analytics information allowed her to track search terms used to locate a guide, and once it was determined that students were seeking statistical resources, the guide was updated to include relevant information, and the success rate for that guide began to improve.[8]

Conclusion

The examples above are a mix of hypothetical and real-world cases, meant to serve as inspiration for where you can take a guide assessment project. As with any project involving technology, the specific capabilities of your system will vary.

You've probably noticed that many, perhaps even most, assessment projects include some combination of techniques. Every assessment technique is more useful for some things than others, and each has its weaknesses, so don't be afraid to mix and match methods to get the information you need.

Notes

1. See especially Candice Dahl, "Electronic Pathfinders in Academic Libraries," *College & Research Libraries* 62, no. 3 (2001): 227–37; Michelle Dalton and Rosalind Pan, "Snakes or Ladders?" *Journal of Academic Librarianship* 40, no. 5 (September 2014): 515–20, doi:10.1016/j.acalib.2014.05.006; Maurice Wakeham, "Library Subject Guides," *Journal of Librarianship & Information Science* 44, no. 3 (September 1, 2012): 199–207; Lora Baldwin and Sue A. McFadden, "Using Statistical Gathering Tools to Determine Effectiveness and Accountability," in *Using LibGuides to Enhance Library Services*, ed. Aaron W. Dobbs, Ryan L. Sittler, and Douglas Cook (Chicago: ALA TechSource, 2013), 191–220; Sharon Whitfield and Claire Clemens, "Showcase of Exceptional LibGuides," in *Using LibGuides to Enhance Library Services*, ed. Aaron W. Dobbs, Ryan L. Sittler, and Douglas Cook (Chicago: ALA TechSource, 2013), 253–88.
2. Beth E. Tumbleson and John J. Burke, *Embedding Librarianship in Learning Management Systems* (Chicago: Neal-Schuman, 2013), 98.
3. Martin P. Courtois, Martha E. Higgins, and Aditya Kapur, "Was This Guide Helpful?" *Reference Services Review* 33, no. 2 (May 2005): 188–96, doi:10.1108/00907320510597381.
4. Dalton and Pan, "Snakes or Ladders?" 518.
5. Mardi Mahaffy, "Student Use of Library Research Guides Following Library Instruction," *Communications in Information Literacy* 6, no. 2 (March 22, 2013): 208, http://www.comminfolit.org/index.php?journal=cil&page=article&op=view&path%5B%5D=v6i2p202&path%5B%5D=156.
6. "Jour 4040 Library Quiz," http://ow.ly/NBEb0.
7. Baldwin and McFadden, "Using Statistical Gathering Tools," 194.
8. Summer Durrant, "Assessing Library Subject Guides Using Google Analytics" (poster presentation, ARL Assessment Conference, Charlottesville, VA, October 29, 2012), https://scholarworks.iupui.edu/handle/1805/3213.

References

Baldwin, Lora, and Sue A. McFadden. "Using Statistical Gathering Tools to Determine Effectiveness and Accountability." In *Using LibGuides to Enhance Library Services: A LITA Guide*, edited by Aaron W. Dobbs, Ryan L. Sittler, and Douglas Cook, 191–220. Chicago: ALA TechSource, an imprint of the American Library Association, 2013.

Courtois, Martin P., Martha E. Higgins, and Aditya Kapur. "Was This Guide Helpful? Users' Perceptions of Subject Guides." *Reference Services Review* 33, no. 2 (May 2005): 188–96. doi:10.1108/00907320510597381.

Dahl, Candice. "Electronic Pathfinders in Academic Libraries: An Analysis of Their Content and Form." *College & Research Libraries* 62, no. 3 (2001): 227–37.

Dalton, Michelle, and Rosalind Pan. "Snakes or Ladders? Evaluating a LibGuides Pilot at UCD Library." *Journal of Academic Librarianship* 40, no. 5 (September 2014): 515–20. doi:10.1016/j.acalib.2014.05.006.

Durrant, Summer. "Assessing Library Subject Guides Using Google Analytics." Poster presentation, ARL Assessment Conference, Charlottesville, VA, October 29, 2012. https://scholarworks.iupui.edu/handle/1805/3213.

Mahaffy, Mardi. "Student Use of Library Research Guides Following Library Instruction." *Communications in Information Literacy* 6, no. 2 (March 22, 2013): 202–13. http://www.comminfolit.org/index.php?journal=cil&page=article&op=view&path%5B%5D=v6i-2p202&path%5B%5D=156.

Tumbleson, Beth E., and John J. Burke. *Embedding Librarianship in Learning Management Systems: A How-to-Do-It Manual for Librarians.* Chicago: Neal-Schuman, an imprint of the American Library Association, 2013.

Wakeham, Maurice. "Library Subject Guides: A Case Study of Evidence-Informed Library Development." *Journal of Librarianship & Information Science* 44, no. 3 (September 1, 2012): 199–207.

Whitfield, Sharon, and Claire Clemens. "Showcase of Exceptional LibGuides." In *Using LibGuides to Enhance Library Services: A LITA Guide*, edited by Aaron W. Dobbs, Ryan L. Sittler, and Douglas Cook, 253–88. Chicago: ALA TechSource, an imprint of the American Library Association, 2013.

CHAPTER 6

Planning, Coordinating, and Administrating Guides

Introduction

MOST OF THIS BOOK to this point has been aimed at the individual guide author, usually an instruction librarian supporting a class or academic subject area. In this final chapter, we'll look at a few of the bigger questions facing instructional planners, managers, or departments.

You and your colleagues will have to make decisions—whether by design or de facto—about how your library operates its research guides, just as with any service point or online resource you offer. It's worthwhile to consider how to make these decisions strategically or at least with an eye toward how they may affect your work down the road.

Remember that a plan should be adjustable; what works well for one library may not for another, so expect to adjust your guide planning and policies based on your own experience, assessment, and feedback from your librarians and users.

Goals

Tying Guide Goals to Instruction Program Goals

A library instruction class has learning objectives that define its specific intent. At a higher level, an instruction *program*—the library's overarching plan for information literacy—has its own defined objectives. Whatever the goals of your individual library's instruction program, a number of these objectives are probably relevant to your research guides.

Consider what problems your instruction program intends to solve that can be addressed by using research guides. In many cases, there won't be anything you can do with guides that's relevant to a specific goal, but with a little creative thought you may be surprised at the applications you can find for them.

Libraries are highly conscious of the need for assessment, and as we saw in chapter 5, including research guides in many assessment projects may be a natural fit. Instruction program goals may suggest useful assessment projects with built-in metrics, and guides can be built with those strategies in mind.

Outreach-related goals often have a place for guides. Guides scale well (one guide can reach a limitless number of students, content can easily be reused and adapted, and so on), they can be embedded in a learning management system, and they can serve populations that may not come to the library in person. Guides can be created for specific campus programs or learning communities related to university initiatives.

Sample Instruction Goals with Research Guide Components

These are some examples of instruction program goals that might be well suited to including research guides, many adapted from or suggested by real-life cases:

- *Library goal:* The library will make resources visible and available to the largest possible number of the university's online students. *Research guide plan:* Place links to library research guides in the university's learning management system (LMS).[1] This could be either an all-purpose template including broadly applicable resources or an individualized approach in which guide content is included in or linked from specific courses or subjects.[2]

- *Library goal:* The library will engage in instructional outreach to the entire incoming first-year class.

  Research guide plan: Create research guides for all sections of a required first-year English composition course. As this is a large population of students with many sections, librarians will design guides with reusable content in mind: tutorials that can be repurposed, instructions that take into account a standardized assignment, and so on.[3]

- *Library goal:* The library will conduct an assessment to determine the level of student satisfaction with library instruction.

  Research guide plan: The assessment instrument will include questions to determine what courses students had had that include library instruction. Librarians will match a list of those classes against a list of existing research guides to see if there is a correlation with the availability of a guide to students' response to instruction.[4]

- *Library goal:* The library will collaborate with a new academic program or campus learning community.[5]

  Research guide plan: Work with faculty collaborators or learning community advisors to identify learning goals of the program or learning community. Most such groups have a subject focus that fits logically into the purview of a subject liaison librarian, who can be tasked with matching the program's goals with relevant library resources and creating a research guide or guides for program participants. This is a good opportunity for faculty-librarian collaboration, and faculty members may be willing to create content for guides as well.

- *Library goal:* The library will contribute to the university's strategic goal of increasing the academic success of students from historically underserved populations.

  Research guide plan: Librarians will use demographic and enrollment data from the university to target guide creation for relevant courses or majors, will research any significant learning characteristics of relevant populations and craft guides appropriately, and will create relevant topical or issue-related guides.

If the populations include disabled persons, particular care will be taken to achieve good accessibility. Librarians will also make a point of including links or guide content for essential skills that may be needed to achieve learning goals in case not all students have received sufficient instruction in the past.[6]

The Research Guide Coordinator

A good way to make sure these goals and questions are not neglected is to designate a coordinator or point person in charge of your library's research guides. There are a number of possibilities for who could fill this role: a front-line instruction librarian, a department head or instruction program coordinator, a member of your IT department, or a paraprofessional staff member, to name a few. Coordinating guides is probably not a full-time job, but it may be a significant responsibility if your librarians are active guide creators, and the best choice depends on what you need this position to do and who your library has available to do it.

The guide coordinator may be responsible for tasks like

- Determining and enforcing policies for guide use.
- Providing training and technical support for guide authors; creating internal documentation for the guide system; troubleshooting technology problems.
- Making design, layout, and creative decisions about the look of the guides and making sure these guidelines are applied consistently.
- Performing administrative and maintenance tasks.
- Generating reports and statistics.

Of course, the best person for this job will vary depending on your institution, and all options may have advantages or disadvantages.

An instruction librarian and experienced guide author understands instructional design elements of guides. They may have a better grasp than IT staff do about how students use guides, and they understand how proposed changes to the guide system will affect authors and users. On the other hand, they may not always be able to solve technical problems without going through vendor support or the IT help desk. Technology may not be the main focus of their job (but then, most guide CMSs don't require extensive technology experience to use).

Having a systems librarian or IT staff member as coordinator has the advantage of putting someone in place who can likely troubleshoot technical problems themselves. They can advise guide authors on HTML, CSS, and web editing. They may have ideas for features that can be enabled that librarians don't know about: creative ways to incorporate data from your catalog or your library's social media feeds, for example. They can probably handle upgrades and installations without need for help from a third party. The disadvantage is that without a grounding in teaching theory, a technical specialist may not understand the needs of individual guide authors. They may not be as comfortable training staff as an instruction librarian would be (though many IT specialists and system librarians are also excellent instructors).

A manager or instruction department head as guide coordinator has the benefit of being able to make some policy decisions—about site design, assessment planning, integration with library-wide goals—and implement them from a higher level of authority than might otherwise be possible. A manager may be able to direct strategic planning of guides in ways that other positions can't. As may be the case in any of these scenarios, though, managing a guide CMS may be more hands-on than many managers can fit into their workload, and delegation must always be an option.

This doesn't all have to be done by one person, of course, and realistically there's probably no one who can do it all completely independently. You may find that the best model for your library is to share responsibilities: have an experienced guide author handling training and design decisions, while handing off troubleshooting and tech support to the library webmaster, while strategic goals are set by the instruction department head. Having a single person designated point of contact often makes things easier for librarians, however, as they always know whom they should ask when they have questions or problems. It may not always be apparent at first whether any given question is one of policy, technology, or training, and having a single coordinator helps cut down on the need to pass around questions to get help.

The successful guide program requires support from all three legs: management, instruction, and technology. Whoever the coordinator and whatever their background, make sure that they have support to fill in whatever gaps might exist: management support to make needed decisions, technical support to maintain and troubleshoot the system, and instructional design and planning support to help chart the role guides play in your library's information literacy program.

Control: How Much Is Too Much?

Inevitably the guide coordinator faces the question of how much to intervene in the design, content, layout, and other elements of guides. Guides on a single library's site are created by a variety of authors, with a range of goals, needs, experience, skills, and approaches.

On one hand, guides represent the public face of the library, and as we've seen in previous chapters, a certain amount of uniformity in visual, navigational, and conceptual design helps students use guides with greater ease and comprehension. On the other hand, guides are teaching tools, and effective teaching requires the teacher to have free rein and make judgment calls based on her own expertise.

In a few areas it's a good idea to maintain control over guide content. This primarily includes visual elements that establish a unified look, feel, and identity for the site, such as

- *Overall color scheme.* It should be obvious when navigating from one guide to the next that all guides are part of the same site, and a consistent color scheme goes a long way in this regard. If most of the site uses the school's colors of red and blue, and a lone-wolf guide author chooses to make his guides black and orange, students may not even recognize that they're still on the library's (or the university's) page.

- *Nonstandard fonts.* To a lesser degree, altering the default fonts on a guide also impacts the feel and identity. Perhaps at least as importantly, using different fonts can make a page less readable and distract from the content. Color is a factor here as well: anything that diverges too far from black text on white is both distracting and more difficult to read. Remember also the discussion of link formatting in chapter 4: blue underlined links are a recognized web convention, and departure from this standard, especially inconsistency, makes the presence of links less clear to the user.

- *Other visual and navigational elements.* This refers to anything *outside* the actual instructional or informational content of an individual guide. Logos, navigational tools such as breadcrumbs (links that help users navigate to previous or top-level pages), menus, and other standardized items established when the guide site is set up should usually be left alone by guide authors.

Depending on your guide CMS, it may be possible for the guide coordinator to lock these elements down and completely prevent guide authors from altering them, or it may be a matter of asking authors to adhere to an agreed-upon policy (and possibly intervening when they stray).

The guide coordinator should be very cautious about interfering with guide content when it comes to anything outside of these standardized factors. If guides are truly to be used as teaching tools, then the coordinator should be hesitant to intervene in matters of content as long as all guides are in line with established policies as suggested above. It is easily possible to establish a look, feel, and visual identity for the guide site while still leaving room for creativity and initiative by guide authors with individual teaching styles! (See the best practices section later in this chapter for some more thoughts.)

Guide Coordinator Case Study

It will come as no surprise to the reader that I serve as research guides coordinator at my library (at a large public university). I initially took on the role almost by chance, because I was hired just as the library was adopting LibGuides several years ago. Since I had some previous experience with the software, I was able to offer training to colleagues as soon as I started. Although I'm primarily a subject librarian, my experience with and interest in managing our guides has been an opportunity that has led me into the larger responsibility of "virtual services librarian," which includes coordinating our online reference service point and has become a significant part of my portfolio.

My responsibilities as guide coordinator include planning and delivering training; managing accounts and guide ownership when librarians arrive, depart, or change positions; making design decisions in consultation with our virtual reference committee; and anything else that seems relevant to the management of our research guides.

I handle front-line tech support requests from my subject librarian colleagues when they encounter problems in the course of working on their guides. These are usually in the nature of figuring out how best to accomplish a desired goal within the features and limitations of the LibGuides software, and as often as not just involve figuring out which buttons to push or whether there's a fault in the HTML code somewhere.

We are fortunate to have a crack digital services department including a web librarian and two programmers, so when I encounter a technical problem that's beyond my limited knowledge of CSS, for example, I can fall back on my colleagues' expertise. I also collaborated extensively with these colleagues during a recent LibGuides upgrade, which required some site redesign, data cleanup, and migrating our guides' URL from the old site to the new one: in short, they took on lots of technically oriented details that were beyond my expertise as an instruction librarian.

Maintenance and Administrative Tasks

The guide coordinator and anyone else involved in administering the library's guides should be prepared to handle (or delegate) many situations. When taking on or assigning responsibilities for your research guides, consider these.

Regular and Periodic Maintenance

Guide authors do a certain amount of maintenance each semester as guides are created, published, unpublished, and revised for each new set of classes. The guide administrator may also need to keep a hand on the tiller in the form of site-wide maintenance, or at least communicate regularly with guide authors.

Links are at the heart of many research guides, and checking and correcting them is important in maintaining guides' usefulness. Many systems like LibGuides have an automatic link checker, which is handy but not a cure-all. Some link checkers check only designated lists of links and may not check links included in body text, so a human eye (and mouse hand) is often still needed. Database subscriptions often come and go, and authors should be notified to remove links to defunct resources.

It may be useful during each semester break to review the list of guides and remove or unpublish guides for courses that won't be taught next term. As we often teach students in info lit sessions, currency of information is an important factor in the usefulness of any website. Pruning the master list of guides keeps it from getting too long to be useful or easily readable and makes it easier for students to find the guide they need. This also applies to any other guides with time-limited usefulness, like outdated current event guides, annual featured books, and pages about library events and workshops that have passed.

Accounts and Ownership

When new instruction librarians arrive, part of the regular new employee checklist should be setting up accounts in the guide system. For the administrator this may also include scheduling and delivering training and reassigning ownership of guides and subject areas.

Likewise, when a librarian departs, remember to assign ownership of their guides and assets to an interim person. While deleting their account may not always be critical (unless there's some risk of an angry former employee taking out their feelings on your research guides!), it's important to make sure that guides have updated contact information for students to get help so that users' e-mail isn't going into the black hole of an abandoned inbox. Don't leave orphaned guides on your public pages.

For this reason, it's a good idea to avoid creating "generic" or departmental accounts in your guide system. Often the library may not want an individual's contact information on a guide, but rather the contact information for a service point like the reference desk, and a simple workaround is to just create an account for the reference desk's e-mail address and assign ownership of the guide to that account. The problem comes down the road when that page needs updating; these generic departmental accounts often slip through the cracks as they're forgotten or their guides neglected. A better policy is to make sure that all guides are assigned to an individual account, and the individual owner's contact information hidden on the page (this is easily done in LibGuides) and replaced with the appropriate service point's contact information.

Consider who has the ability to edit and make changes to others' guides. The library's webmaster? The guide coordinator? Department heads? Support staff or student assistants? There are cases in which any or all of these people may need to collaborate on a guide or make updates in a colleague's absence. Consider carefully before granting anyone administrative access to the entire site; it's often possible and preferable to give individuals the ability to share access to specific guides or sections rather than handing out admin accounts with too much abandon. This isn't to suggest mistrust of colleagues; it's just sensible to limit the authority to alter or take down a library-wide service point.

Collecting and Reporting Data

Assessment is king, and as discussed in the previous chapter, usage data is a relatively simple starting point for assessing research guides.

Plan ahead for possible future assessment, in conjunction with management and any stakeholders in your library's assessment work or annual reports. Determine what data you might want or need down the line, and decide whether it might be useful or necessary to generate periodic reports monthly or on some other schedule. An annual report may be all you need, or if creating reports is complicated or difficult in your system, you may want to create smaller regular reports more frequently rather than doing it all at once.

Examine the capabilities of your guide CMS to generate usage statistics. If the built-in features are insufficient for what you think you may need in the future, talk to your webmaster early on about setting up Google Analytics, since it's not able to generate retroactive reports.

Upgrading and Overhauling

From time to time, most online systems and software, including the guides' CMS, will need some kind of major maintenance. This may be a software version upgrade, migrating guides or content from one platform to another, an overhaul of your database system requiring a massive link-editing project, or something else.

This is a good chance for the guide coordinator to flex her project management muscles, or acquire some. This kind of project can end up affecting many librarians and users, so be prepared, keep track of everything, and communicate a lot.

Start planning projects like this early so you have time to plan and delegate all the tasks and sub-tasks involved. Ideally, major upgrades or changes should take place during a semester break or summer when they're less likely to affect students. No one wants to deal with panicking students who can't get the info they need when an assignment is coming due. Allow some extra time in the project schedule for things to go wrong; hopefully you won't need it.

Think carefully about what departments of the library are affected by a change to the guides system. Guide authors may include not only instruction and subject librarians but also circulation, archives, or other departments that create content for students and faculty. Your IT department and web librarian will almost certainly involved and may be key players supporting the project. Other departments could conceivably be involved, including electronic resources librarians, possibly cataloging (e.g., if your guides appear in your OPAC), and anyone else who links to library resources.

Communicate with managers in those affected departments first. Ask them about any implications you hadn't thought of, get their suggestions for people in their departments to work with you for the support you need, and get their advice in crafting e-mails you're sending out to notify your colleagues. Keep them up-to-date on how it's going, especially if you encounter problems.

If you need guide authors to participate directly—updating links, making backups of their content, or otherwise spending their time in support of the upgrade or overhaul—let them know early. If this is a venture that's going to take significant time, allow colleagues enough advance warning to fit it into their schedules and the academic calendar.

Consider any auxiliary work that may be useful to do at the same time. It's rare that we get the opportunity to step back and look at the big picture of some of our services and systems, and it may be a good chance to do some spring cleaning. If you're migrating to a new platform, for example, think about running a report to identify any least-used, out-of-date, or long-unpublished guides. Do they need to be migrated to the new CMS, or is this a good time to clear them out of the system?

Training

Unless you have a completely home-grown system, you don't need to plan training from scratch. There's a great deal of training material available for most guide CMSs. This is especially true for LibGuides, as (currently) the most popular library guide system, but a web search for most systems will reveal videos, handouts, and workshop outlines—created by the vendor or by other librarians—that can be used as-is or adapted.

Instruction librarians already know the basics of creating good training: the same principles apply to training peers as teaching an undergraduate class. Spend some time deciding on some specific learning objectives. Most likely, guide authors being trained will not need to know nearly as much about the system as the guide coordinator does.

They'll need to know how to accomplish specific tasks like creating new guides; editing content, including adding media elements like images and videos; performing some basic maintenance functions like publishing and unpublishing guides, editing metadata fields like titles and subject headings; and so on.

Eliminate anything from the training that's not likely to come up in guide authors' day-to-day work. For example, if your documentation includes instructions for creating accounts, adjusting system-wide colors, and posting announcements on the guide home page, eliminate it from anything you're handing out to authors and create a shorter version. Anything that's highly technical or oriented for system administrators should go—keep learning objectives relevant to the audience's information needs, as always, and throw out anything that's not.

Gariepy et al. offer more detailed advice, including
- Offer training options in a variety of formats.
- Evaluate what type of documentation will work best—vendor-created or customized—depending on factors including how much time can be invested in keeping it updated.
- Address the specific needs of guide authors, including concerns and skepticism, and provide personalized support.
- Tie training to library-specific goals and user needs.[7]

If you're training colleagues whom you know well, use that knowledge—and the discussion of learning styles from chapter 3—as you plan training sessions. Plan exercises and training activities just as you would for students. (One study shows that instruction and reference librarians may have a slight preference for verbal over visual learning, and for active rather than reflective learning.[8])

Training can offer a good opportunity not only to teach colleagues the features of your guides' CMS and what button to click to insert an image, but also to go a little deeper. It can also be the time to have some discussion about some of the elements of good design: addressing instructional objectives, planning visual structure, and achieving good user experience in order to encourage students to use research guides. This is the kind of thing—incorporating institution-specific content—that can't be done solely with generic or vendor-created training materials, and it's worth putting a little thought and effort into when planning training.

As important as providing good training to begin with, is making sure that guide authors have someone to follow up with for help and questions afterward. Training is important, but there will always be situations that don't come up until later, during hands-on use. Make a note (at least a mental one) of follow-up questions that come up frequently during training sessions, and add them to the next round of documentation and training.

Extending Your Reach

Increasing the visibility of guides and the amount of guide use are common goals for libraries. Creating guides is wasted effort if no one actually uses them. In chapter 5 we looked at some means of assessment that can be used to get a better idea of who is using your guides and how much. If you've done that and determined that your guides are not being used to their full potential, what can you do about it?

Classroom Instruction

Multiple studies have shown that one of the most effective ways to encourage use of research guides is to use them in face-to-face classes:

> Close inspection of statistics revealed a direct causal relationship between in-person instruction and the number of visits to subject research guides. The more a librarian teaches, the more their guide will be used regardless of whether they instruct students to visit the site during a library workshop.[9]

> Students who received library instruction … tended to use subject guide pages more frequently. A statistically significant correlation was found between attendance at library instruction sessions and the reported frequency of using [research guides].[10]

> Our usage statistics indicate that it is not simply enough to create and post a guide; it is also necessary to promote

> it in some way, or preferably, multiple ways…. [A spike
> in guide usage] is reflected in … guides that were used in
> class sessions…. The positive implication for this trend
> is that if students are shown where a guide can be found
> and how to use it, they will return.[11]

If the guide has been designed with the assignment in mind, as we've
discussed in chapter 2, then using it as an in-class teaching aid comes naturally. Showing students in class how to get to the guide (and that it exists)
and stressing that it contains resources and links that they will need may be
one of the best and simplest plans to increase guide usage.

Make Guides Findable

Make sure your students can locate the guide they need and recognize it
as relevant when they do. Choose keywords and titles carefully and with
a user's perspective in mind. Labeling guides clearly and specifically will
make them more search engine-friendly and make it easier for students to
spot what they need. Remember that students, especially undergraduates,
may not recognize a general subject guide as relevant to them, but will
certainly gravitate more strongly to a guide labeled with their course and
professor's name.

Keep guides' content relevant to promote their continued use. *Relevant*
certainly means different things to different libraries. Guides that relate to
current events, hot research topics, and campus programming can be useful and fun and help drive web traffic to your guides. The one topic guar-
anteed to be relevant to students, of course, is this semester's assignment.

Faculty Outreach

Faculty will always have access to students' ears. Don't overlook the obvious: for subject liaisons, occasionally notifying your faculty of a new or
useful guide will help increase guide use and encourage faculty to promote guides to their classes. Include mentions of research guides in any
periodic "check-in" or "touching base" e-mails or newsletters you may already be sending to your departments. Many faculty may not be aware
of the existence of library research guides, so even if the specific guides
you're promoting aren't useful for their classes, it still serves to raise their

awareness of guides as a library service and may result in requests for new guides. Studies find that this simple outreach technique tends to result in enthusiastic e-mail and a significant increase in use of the specific guides promoted.[12]

Social Media

Most libraries have some sort of presence on social media, at least a Facebook page or Twitter account. Promoting guides on your social sites can be a great way to feature library resources in a fun and interesting way. My library regularly schedules themed posts on specific days of the week: Throwback Thursday featuring historic or archival resources, Today We Learned featuring weird or intriguing facts supported by research sources, and Space and Services promoting useful hints about resources available in the library. Any of these ideas could easily feature research guides.

Use what you know about your social media audience to select featured guides. Targeting a particular stakeholder population (based on need, library initiatives, or other factors) is often a useful strategy, and content targeted at one group often holds interest for other groups as well.[13]

Reach out to other departments on campus to encourage sharing and cross-posting each other's links and posts to get a wider audience for guides. If you're sharing a research guide about sports medicine, tag the athletics department's Facebook profile. When you feature a Black History Month guide, add the African American Student Alliance's Twitter handle to your post.

Library Website

Work with your web librarian to determine where best to feature guides on your website. Be sure not to bury your guides too deeply within the library's site.[14] The fewer clicks students need to get there from the homepage, the more likely they are to use them. One click from the homepage is good; two clicks is iffy; three clicks probably means students won't get there from here.

If you have rotating content on your homepage—promotions for featured services, blog posts, or anything along these lines—this can be a useful place to promote guides. Remember that every fall brings a new audience. Use your knowledge of semester-based research peaks to time promotions of guides on your website: at my library, two to three weeks into the semester (when students receive term paper assignments) and about two weeks before its end (when many students get serious about research with due dates coming up) are prime times.

Your Mileage May Vary

Don't forget to build assessment into your promotion and marketing of guides (simply tracking trends in page hits is probably sufficient) to figure out what's working and what's not. A lot will depend on your library's and institution's environment. The results may surprise you: a study by Foster et al. reported that featuring guides on the library's homepage, contrary to the advice about requiring fewer clicks, resulted in almost no increase in guide usage.[15]

Reuse, Reduce, Recycle

Librarians may find it difficult and time-consuming to create guides for every need, but students show a higher level of engagement with guides customized to their individual courses and assignments. This can be a difficult predicament to resolve. One way to address it is by encouraging an institutional culture of content sharing among guide authors. Reusing and adapting existing guide content—your own and other librarians'—helps creators get more use from guides without overextending their available time and effort. Do what you can to make creating and sharing guide content easy, both technically and administratively speaking.

While students recognize and appreciate guides that are based on their specific assignment, this doesn't mean that every single course guide has to be created individually from scratch. Many courses and assignments within the same discipline are similar enough—from the point of view of library research resources—that it's often a more efficient use of time to copy one of your existing guides, use it as a template, and then customize the details than to start from a blank slate each time. (If your CMS doesn't have a built-in "reuse content" feature like LibGuides, copying and pasting is easy.)

There are plenty of exceptions and special cases, and this isn't a practical strategy all the time, but consider whether each new guide has some common elements with an existing one: a catalog search section, research strategy advice, links to databases, and so on. Even if the sophomore literature research paper uses only half the same elements as the first-year assignment, it may be faster and easier to copy that guide and then adjust the guide to the stages of the new assignment.

Some libraries use a repository of learning objects and instructional content: digital objects like tutorials, figures and images, instructions and help for library services like interlibrary loan and off-campus access, and so on. Such a resource can also help reluctant guide authors get their feet wet:

> Having a digital learning object repository also helps librarians new to embedded librarianship by providing ready-made content. This content can often be customized to reflect class-specific examples.... By providing ready-made online instructional content instead of requiring each embedded librarian to create his or her own content, the digital learning object repository can reduce concerns about the time and technological skills required for online embedded librarianship and potentially encourage more librarians to get involved.[16]

The guide coordinator may be able to provide a pool of content like this by creating template guides to pull from, shared among guide authors on an intranet or back end of the CMS, and available for guide authors to make contributions, but not visible to the public. Even a shared network drive would do. This doesn't have to be a literal shared repository, though—having one's own guides to pull from can often be a sufficiently useful personal repository after the librarian has created a year or two's worth of guides, and most guide authors engage in some form of this practice.

Libraries have been doing this for years with the concept of the "instruction menu," a selection of suggested concepts and topics available to cover during in-person class sessions.[17] Some libraries offer this sort of menu for the information of faculty members who are scheduling library classes to give them an idea of what's available for their students. This doesn't mean that the content of our instruction sessions is modular or mindlessly interchangeable—these are topics that we frequently cover that we adapt to the needs of each class. In the same way, copying and adapting content doesn't mean we're cheaping out or taking short cuts. It's an acknowledgment that, as we do in the classroom, we often build guides on material we've taught before as a starting point to adapt and tailor to the next class's need.

Encourage a culture of sharing among library colleagues. As your library establishes best practices for creating and managing your research guides, discuss the idea of copying content from one another's guides. Decide whether it's appropriate or necessary to ask permission of the original creator before copying or adapting their work, or whether you agree that it's acceptable to reuse content—possibly including a credit and/or a link to the original guide (figure 6.1).

Credit Statement Linking to Original Guide

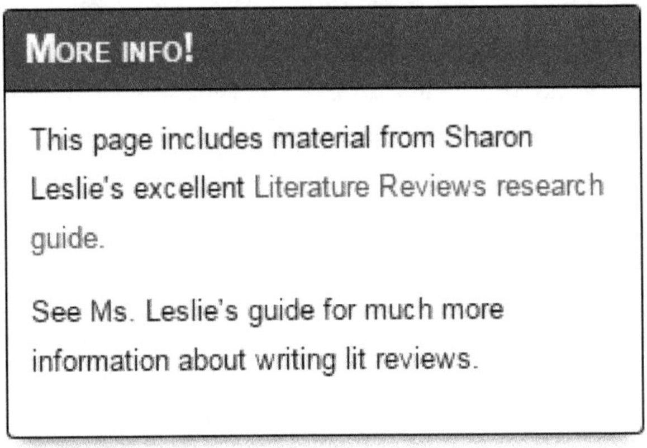

MORE INFO!

This page includes material from Sharon Leslie's excellent Literature Reviews research guide.

See Ms. Leslie's guide for much more information about writing lit reviews.

FIGURE 6.1

I copied and adapted a page from a colleague's guide that I liked (with her permission), saving myself a lot of work. This statement credits her work and links back to her original guide.

Finally, consider whether you will give permission for other libraries to use your work on their own guides. One way to provide blanket permission is by adding a Creative Commons license statement to your guides (figure 6.2). In effect, this is a preemptive permission statement meaning "Yes, you may copy this guide as long as I'm credited on your derivative work." My own guides include a CC license, and one of my guides that is widely copied across the web—the one I created for Zotero several years ago—results in a great deal of public awareness of my work and many links back to my original guide page, which in turn boosts the guide in Google search results.

Creative Commons License

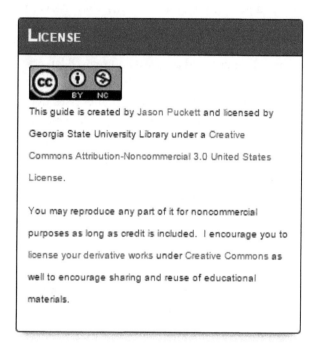

LICENSE

This guide is created by Jason Puckett and licensed by Georgia State University Library under a Creative Commons Attribution-Noncommercial 3.0 United States License.

You may reproduce any part of it for noncommercial purposes as long as credit is included. I encourage you to license your derivative works under Creative Commons as well to encourage sharing and reuse of educational materials.

FIGURE 6.2

A sample Creative Commons license on a guide, granting other libraries permission to copy and adapt the guide as long as they credit the original author.

You may need to check with your institution's legal affairs office before making any statement of copyright permission on your guide pages, but licensing and sharing work in this way is becoming more and more common practice. (See http://creativecommons.org for more information about CC licenses.)

Don't be shy about asking other libraries for permission to copy their guides. As long as credit is included, this is not unlike the culture of citation with which academic librarians are already comfortable, and I've never had a librarian decline permission when I've e-mailed to ask.

Establishing Best Practices

Above all, it's a good idea to get everyone in your library on the same page about your approach to making and maintaining guides. If you're establishing procedures and guidelines, give librarians a say in determining them, and share the rationale for any decisions. Collect any established standards in a best practices document so that it can be shared transparently, commented upon by colleagues, and assessed and revised later.

The best practices document published by Gonzalez and Westbrock of New Mexico State University (figure 6.3) addresses questions of purpose (needs, buy-in, and publicity/marketing), audience awareness (the need for accessibility, regular use and positive user experience), assessment (data tracking, user feedback, and assessment planning and sharing), faculty collaboration (information gathering, communication with course instructors, link placement), and maintenance (staffing and oversight).[18]

Figure 6.3 NMSU Best Practices

LibGuides Best Practices, New Mexico State University Library

Throughout the process of transferring online guides to the LibGuides platform, the project leaders kept a working list of best practices taking into consideration all the challenges, benefits, and lessons encountered. Access to the NMSU Library's collection of guides is at: http://libguides.nmsu.edu.

Purpose, organization, planning

- Articulate problems with current situation and be specific in identifying specific organization needs.
- Establish buy-in with involved parties (administration, reference department, systems department, etc.).
- Plan for dissemination both internally (e.g., training) and externally (e.g., placement, naming, and marketing).

Audience awareness

- Make guides accessible to users at their point of need and point of access (e.g., course management systems).
- Use guides consistently in library instruction and in reference transactions.
- Create a consistent look and feel.

Evaluation and assessment

- Monitor the use of guides.
- Create a policy for adding/deleting guides.
- Solicit user feedback.
- Create an assessment plan.
- Share assessment with involved parties (administration, reference department, systems department, etc.).

Faculty collaboration

- Collect syllabi and create course/assignment guides.
- Use guides as basis for communication and collaboration.
- Embed links to guides in course management systems.

Maintenance

- Use available resources (e.g., student workers)
- Maintain an inventory of guides.
- Identify long-term editors who will oversee the entire collection of guides.

It's simple and adaptable, providing guidelines but not detailed procedures for every case. This is all you need. Notice that a number of stakeholders are called out for their relevance to specific areas: administration, systems, reference. Some elements are explicitly left open and flexible and are not yet finalized: creating a policy for adding and deleting guides and creating an assessment plan are named as work to be done in the future.

Other practices that could be included at an institution with different needs might include things like

- encouraging copying content between guides
- protocols for creating guides for non-instructional purposes: when should a page be a guide, and when should it go on the main body of the library site?
- specifics of look and feel: fonts and colors
- suggestions for user experience aspects
- job expectations for guide authors, how guide creation will be assessed in annual reviews

Don't get bogged down in too many details, though. This is big-picture planning intended to provide long-term guidance to guide authors and the coordinators.

Keep your best practices simple, get buy-in from guide authors, and be prepared to update them as you learn and as circumstances change. Keep your institutional and departmental goals in mind as you craft your best practices document: use these goals to inform your practices, and use both to guide you toward an assessment plan, which in turn can feed back into suggesting the next revision of goals and practices.

Notes

1. Aaron Bowen, "A LibGuides Presence in a Blackboard Environment," *Reference Services Review* 40, no. 3 (2012): 449–68, doi:10.1108/00907321211254698.
2. Beth E. Tumbleson and John Burke, *Embedding Librarianship in Learning Management Systems* (Chicago: Neal-Schuman, 2013), 120; Leslie G. Adebonojo, "LibGuides," *College & Undergraduate Libraries* 17, no. 4 (December 2010): 398–412, doi:10.1080/10691316.2010.525426.
3. Matthew C. Sylvain et al., "Reusable Learning Objects," in *Teaching Information Literacy Online*, ed. Thomas P. Mackey and Trudy Jacobson (New York: Neal-Schuman, 2011), 25–45.
4. Melissa Bowles-Terry, "Library Instruction and Academic Success," *Evidence Based Library and Information Practice* 7, no. 1 (March 9, 2012): 90.
5. David Lavoie, Andrew Rosman, and Shikha Sharma, "Information Literacy by Design," in *Teaching Information Literacy Online*, ed. Thomas P. Mackey and Trudy Jacobson (New York: Neal-Schuman, 2011), 133–58; Joyce Lindstrom and Diana D. Shonrock, "Faculty-Librarian Collaboration to Achieve

Integration of Information Literacy," *Reference & User Services Quarterly* 46, no. 1 (October 1, 2006): 18–23.

6. Earnestine Adeyemon, "Integrating Digital Literacies into Outreach Services for Underserved Youth Populations," *Reference Librarian* 50, no. 1 (January 2009): 85–98, doi:10.1080/02763870802546423.

7. Laura Westmoreland Gariepy et al., "Developing LibGuides Training," in *Using LibGuides to Enhance Library Services*, ed. Aaron W. Dobbs, Ryan L. Sittler, and Douglas Cook (Chicago: ALA TechSource, 2013).

8. Amanda Rinehart, Jennifer Sharkey, and Chad Kahl, "Learning Style Dimensions and Professional Characteristics of Academic Librarians," *College & Research Libraries* 76, no. 4 (May 2015): 460–62, doi:10.5860/crl.76.4.450.

9. Mira Foster et al., "Marketing Research Guides," *Journal of Library Administration* 50, no. 5–6 (2010): 608.

10. Shannon M. Staley, "Academic Subject Guides," *College & Research Libraries* 68, no. 2 (March 2007): 129.

11. Rachel McMullin and Jane Hutton, "Web Subject Guides," *Journal of Library Administration* 50, no. 7/8 (December 2010): 793, doi:10.1080/01930826.2010.488972.

12. Ibid.; Foster et al., "Marketing Research Guides," 611.

13. Sarah K. Steiner, *Strategic Planning for Social Media in Libraries* (Chicago: ALA TechSource, 2012), 34–35.

14. Candice Dahl, "Electronic Pathfinders in Academic Libraries," *College & Research Libraries* 62, no. 3 (2001): 237.

15. Foster et al., "Marketing Research Guides," 609.

16. Danielle Skaggs, "Using a Digital Learning Object Repository to Provide Library Support for Online Learning," in *Embedded Librarianship*, ed. Alice Daugherty and Michael F. Russo (Santa Barbara, CA: ABC-CLIO, 2013), 87, http://public.eblib.com/choice/publicfullrecord.aspx?p=1489951.

17. Tumbleson and Burke, *Embedding Librarianship in Learning Management Systems*, 48, has a great example.

18. Alisa C. Gonzalez and Theresa Westbrock, "Reaching Out with LibGuides," *Journal of Library Administration* 50, no. 5/6 (July 2010): 656, doi:10.1080/01930826.2010.488941.

References

Adebonojo, Leslie G. "LibGuides: Customizing Subject Guides for Individual Courses." *College & Undergraduate Libraries* 17, no. 4 (December 2010): 398–412. doi:10.1080/10691316.2010.525426.

Adeyemon, Earnestine. "Integrating Digital Literacies into Outreach Services for Underserved Youth Populations." *Reference Librarian* 50, no. 1 (January 2009): 85–98. doi:10.1080/02763870802546423.

Bowen, Aaron. "A LibGuides Presence in a Blackboard Environment." *Reference Services Review* 40, no. 3 (2012): 449–68. doi:10.1108/00907321211254698.

Bowles-Terry, Melissa. "Library Instruction and Academic Success: A Mixed-Methods Assessment of a Library Instruction Program." *Evidence Based Library and Information Practice* 7, no. 1 (March 9, 2012): 82–95.

Dahl, Candice. "Electronic Pathfinders in Academic Libraries: An Analysis of Their Content and Form." *College & Research Libraries* 62, no. 3 (2001): 227–37.

Foster, Mira, Hesper Wilson, Nicole Allensworth, and Diane T. Sands. "Marketing Research Guides: An Online Experiment with LibGuides." *Journal of Library Administration* 50, no. 5–6 (2010): 602–16.

Gariepy, Laura Westmoreland, Emily S. Mazure, Jennifer A. McDaniel, and Erin R. White. "Developing LibGuides Training: A Blended-Learning Approach." In *Using LibGuides to Enhance Library Services: A LITA Guide*, edited by Aaron W. Dobbs, Ryan L. Sittler, and Douglas Cook, 85–100. Chicago: ALA TechSource, an imprint of the American Library Association, 2013.

Gonzalez, Alisa C., and Theresa Westbrock. "Reaching Out with LibGuides: Establishing a Working Set of Best Practices." *Journal of Library Administration* 50, no. 5/6 (July 2010): 638–56. doi:10.1080/01930826.2010.488941.

Lavoie, David, Andrew Rosman, and Shikha Sharma. "Information Literacy by Design: Recalibrating Graduate Professional Asynchronous Online Programs." In *Teaching Information Literacy Online*, edited by Thomas P. Mackey and Trudi Jacobson, 133–58. New York: Neal-Schuman, 2011.

Lindstrom, Joyce, and Diana D. Shonrock. "Faculty-Librarian Collaboration to Achieve Integration of Information Literacy." *Reference & User Services Quarterly* 46, no. 1 (October 1, 2006): 18–23.

McMullin, Rachel, and Jane Hutton. "Web Subject Guides: Virtual Connections across the University Community." *Journal of Library Administration* 50, no. 7/8 (December 2010): 789–97. doi:10.1080/01930826.2010.488972.

Rinehart, Amanda, Jennifer Sharkey, and Chad Kahl. "Learning Style Dimensions and Professional Characteristics of Academic Librarians." *College & Research Libraries* 76, no. 4 (May 2015): 450–68. doi:10.5860/crl.76.4.450.

Skaggs, Danielle. "Using a Digital Learning Object Repository to Provide Library Support for Online Learning." In *Embedded Librarianship: What Every Academic Librarian Should Know*, edited by Alice Daugherty and Michael

F. Russo, 85–98. Santa Barbara, CA: ABC-CLIO, 2013. http://public.eblib.com/choice/publicfullrecord.aspx?p=1489951.

Staley, Shannon M. "Academic Subject Guides: A Case Study of Use at San José State University." *College & Research Libraries* 68, no. 2 (March 2007): 119–39.

Steiner, Sarah K. *Strategic Planning for Social Media in Libraries.* Chicago: ALA TechSource, an imprint of the American Library Association, 2012.

Sylvain, Matthew C., Kari Mofford, Elizabeth Lehr, and Jeannette E. Riley. "Reusable Learning Objects: Developing Online Information Literacy Instruction through Collaborative Design." In *Teaching Information Literacy Online*, edited by Thomas P. Mackey and Trudi Jacobson, 25–45. New York: Neal-Schuman, 2011.

Tumbleson, Beth E., and John Burke. *Embedding Librarianship in Learning Management Systems: A How-to-Do-It Manual for Librarians.* Chicago: Neal-Schuman, an imprint of the American Library Association, 2013.

Author Biography

Jason Puckett is Librarian for Communication and Virtual Services and Assistant Professor at Georgia State University Library in Atlanta, Georgia. He was named a *Library Journal* Mover and Shaker in 2010, in part for his work with technology in libraries.

Puckett has a BA in English from Georgia State University and an MLIS from Florida State University. He has worked in libraries for over 20 years and has been teaching for the last 15 of those. He teaches professional workshops on research guides and other topics for Simmons College School of Library and Information Science and has previously co-produced a long-running podcast about information literacy instruction. For several years he's been researching and speaking about how to make research guides better based on the principles in this book.